TOTAL HEALING

Trevor Dearing, MA, BD

Mohr Books

Printed by ColourBooks Ltd, Baldoyle, Dublin 13.

© *Mohr Books*, 1998

Published by Mohr Books
345 Old Birmingham Road
Bromsgrove
B60 1NX

ISBN   0 9524604 6 7

British Library Cataloguing in Publication Data.
A catalogue record for this book is available from the British Library.

By the same author:

Supernatural Superpowers (Logos/Bridge USA)
Supernatural Healing Today (Logos/Bridge USA*)*
God and Healing of the Mind (Bridge/Valley)
A People of Power (Marshall Collins)
It's True! (Mohr Books)

Also published by *Mohr Books*:

The Kentle-Shaddy by Eileen Mohr (novel for children aged 8-12)
The Essential Book of Recipes for Good Living Eileen Mohr
A Well Brought Up Eastender E.H.(Ernie) Relf

This book is dedicated to my six grandsons:
Mark, James, Daniel, Matthew, Daniel and Mark

Contents

Preface

I had been a Christian only a few months before I encountered Hainault. Converted at the age of thirty-one after a traditional boarding school experience of Church, I very soon came to suspect that it could and should be a place of more reality than I had yet found. Was there no current experience in the Church of the things I had read about in Acts?

Through a City contact I made my first visit to St Paul's, Hainault, on one of those wonderful Tuesday evenings. Acts was right there, happening all around me! This was different from anything I had seen before. There was joy, there was expectancy – and life. God was clearly meeting with His people, saving, healing, empowering, freeing and blessing. The reality was almost tangible; the Lord Himself was there.

I was immediately impressed by Trevor's naturalness, joy and deep personal devotion to Jesus. Here was no stuffy cleric but a humble man whose faith and joy were infectious. I was struck by the overt and 'public' character of his ministry as was the ministry of Jesus Himself. People were interviewed, glad to disclose how and why they had changed. The desire for healing of a person particularly in need was shared with the whole congregation so that all could join in ministry to them. Invitations to respond to the message preached required overt action to be taken in front of everyone else as people stood or walked forward. The result was a deeper reality, expectancy and sense of corporeity.

Trevor has had a profound effect on my ministry and has been an invaluable model. His humour, devotion and faith have always been an inspiration. It has been a privilege to learn from him, minister with him, receive his guidance and be his friend.

Chris Oldroyd
Pastor of the Vineyard Church, Farnham, Surrey.

Introduction

This book is meant to be a companion volume to the one which fully describes my life and ministry, for instance how I was called and equipped for Divine healing ministry, and especially how I saw God move in power at my parish church of St Paul, Hainault, on the outskirts of London. That book is called *It's True!*. It was also published by Mohr Books and is available from the publisher, myself, or Christian bookshops.

Although the present book is full of teaching from the Bible and about my own ministry, I must point out that my wonderful wife Anne, to whom I have been married for over forty years, has been my constant companion, support, and partner in all my ministry. She is wonderfully gifted by God in the realm of healing, and has a glorious testimony to give about her conversion, baptism in the Holy Spirit and the way in which God has used her in all the gifts of the Spirit. We have four children, all now mature adults and Christians with whom we share deep love and fellowship. We also have, at present, six grandsons who love the Lord.

I want to thank my editor Eileen Mohr for her very helpful suggestions and for publishing this my eighth book. I believe it contains the very best of the teaching I have given in the previous seven, most of which are now out of print.

Anne and I are still actively engaged in ministry and are open to invitations from churches of all denominations to conduct evangelistic/healing/renewal meetings or teaching seminars. We hope to see even more of God's power at work in the total healing of spirit, mind and body as we practise what we preach until the Lord returns or calls us home.

T.D.

Prologue

I was myself healed by God at the age of nineteen, when I didn't even know Him or give Him any thought. It was a deed of His grace; His sheer undeserved love in action. I had had my first terrible panic attack at the age of eleven, and these dreadful feelings of terror became daily occurrences. They developed also into what are now called 'phobias'. I was terrified of dying; terrified of living; terrified of going insane; terrified of going blind; terrified of going out of the house and terrified of going to school.

At the age of twelve I was so deep in depression that I sat with my head between my knees unable to communicate with anyone. I eventually developed paranoia, believing that the doctor and even my parents were trying to poison me. I lay awake night after night trembling and sweating with fear. I dreaded the nights even more than the frightening days. I was not at home in this world. I wished I had never been born into such a fearful place. This serious mental illness went on and on.

Because this happened to me at an age when there is considerable physical growth, I developed a bent back and walked with a stoop. I was painfully thin, had an ashen white face with black rings around my eyes, and eventually was covered with hideous spots and boils. I had to make regular visits to a heart specialist, and even developed tuberculosis. At the age of eighteen I was instantly rejected as being very unfit for National Service in the armed forces, and a doctor declared that I would only be suitable for light office work as long as I lived. My life expectancy, he added, was twenty-five years. It seemed I had no future and would never be able to take responsibility for a wife and family. My situation was grim indeed.

At the age of nineteen I sat for the first time in a church that happened to be a Methodist Church, which my sister Audrey was attending. We had not been in any way a church-going family. I sat near the door of the church as I always had, even at home, so as to feel I could escape and run somewhere – although I never knew where I would run to. As I sat there I understood nothing of the Service. Eventually, however, the minister, Reverend William Watts, said:

"Jesus promised: 'Come unto me all who labour and are heavy laden and I will give you rest. Take my yoke upon you and learn of me; for I am meek and lowly in heart: and you will find rest unto your souls. For my yoke is easy, and my burden is light.' "

It was the word 'rest' which struck deep into my mind because, for as long as I could remember, I had never known any rest for my tormented being.

"Jesus," I whispered, "if you really are alive as this man says, please help me, because I have no hope."

Immediately I felt overwhelmed with what I vaguely recognised as 'peace'. My whole body glowed warm. Jesus somehow became real, and I was excited. I became a Christian there and then; and within six weeks I was totally healed, emotionally and physically, of all my sicknesses. This was, I now see in retrospect, my introduction to Jesus, the Healer.

In due course I felt called to the ministry, first of the Methodist, then the Anglican Church. I studied at Cliff Bible College in Derbyshire; Wesley Theological College in Headingley, Leeds, and Queen's College, Birmingham, where I obtained honours degrees in Theology.

I served the Church in Brighouse (Yorkshire), Todmorden (Lancashire), Silkstone, near Barnsley and Northowram near Halifax, in which places I exercised a rather liberal, middle of the road, sincere but un-spectacular ministry. I prayed for the sick in their absence and always added, "If it be Thy will, O Lord"; but had no specific healing ministry.

Then, in 1969, my wife Anne's brother George became distressingly ill with cancer. We met an Anglican clergyman, Rev John Tyndale-Biscoe, who said that he knew of a pastor who ministered to the sick at a Pentecostal Church in Welwyn Garden City. I was reluctant to go to a church of this kind, but Anne's desperate concern for her brother took her to a service there. She was so impressed by what she saw and heard there, that when she related these things to me, my curiosity was aroused, and I decided to go along with her on her next visit.

I sat in the Assembly of God Church some weeks later, highly sceptical of the teaching the pastor gave about divine healing, until I saw a lady, on whom he had laid hands, get up out of her wheelchair and walk, having been, we were told, fourteen years in a completely paralysed condition. I was amazed.

At the end of the service I asked the pastor, Lewis Adcock, where his secret source of power lay.

"In the baptism of the Holy Spirit," he replied.

"Can I receive this power?" I enquired.

"You can if you are born again," he promised.

*In brief, I received this wonderful blessing on 10th May 1969 and I knew that my spiritual life had been filled with the same power in a similar way to that of the apostles on the Day of Pentecost.

I subsequently went, with Anne and the children, to be the vicar of a very small church down the back streets of a London housing estate; this was St Paul's Church,

*All the details of my life and ministry can be discovered by reading my book, *It's True!*, published by **Mohr Books** 1996.

Hainault. I had only a very few members, mainly elderly, in my congregation. I took them in a minibus to the Pentecostal church in Welwyn Garden City; with them was a young lady called Carol whose marriage was in ruins. She was suffering from a terrible mental breakdown.

At the appropriate time, Pastor Adcock called the sick forward for prayer and, to my astonishment, publicly announced that *I* would minister to them! I was very hesitant but felt that I could do nothing but obey. I closed my eyes and laid my hands on Carol's head, and discovered, to my great surprise, that she had fallen to the floor. The nine others likewise seemingly collapsed. Then Carol announced that she had been completely healed. The others did so too. My healing ministry had begun!

We began "Power, Praise and Healing" services at St Paul's Church on a Tuesday evening, and soon many miracles of conversion, baptism in the Holy Spirit, healing of mind and body, and even deliverance from evil spirits began to take place. These events were related in every national newspaper, on radio and eventually television. The church became packed with six hundred people, and folk formed queues at four o'clock in the afternoon to be sure of being able to get into the church. This phenomenon continued until 1975.

I was eventually asked to take this ministry all over the British Isles, and even to the Diocese of Singapore. Meanwhile, Anne had also become involved in the healing ministry alongside myself. In September 1975, the Bishop of Chelmsford, Rt Rev John Trillo, sent for me and told me that I should leave St Paul's for a worldwide 'faith' ministry to all denominations. Anne and I, except for the years pastoring St Luke's Episcopal Church, Seattle USA 1981-1983, and except for times of rest and recuperation, have been "on the road" – living by faith and exercising our Gospel-Healing ministry ever since, in accordance with the strength the Lord has given us.

PART ONE

A Biblical Study

Note: Biblical quotations are usually from the New International Version. Occasionally they are from the New American Standard Version (*NASV*) or the King James, Authorised Version (*AV*).

Chapter 1
Suffering and the sovereignty of God

This world is not as God intended it to be. Genesis Chapter 1 verse 31 reads:

*And God saw all that He had made, and **it was very good.***

This text indicates that the earth was made a perfect environment in which mankind could live out his life. The Bible declares that our Creator made a wonderful world, where all was harmony – mankind living in a perfect ecological system alongside the animals, birds and vegetation; everything in balance, just as He had placed the moon in exactly the optimum position between the sun and the earth to produce the ocean tides, so that their ebb and flow give excellent habitats for myriads of different kinds of wildlife.

Whether you see Genesis Chapters 2 and 3 as literal truth or allegorical truth, you cannot fail to appreciate the premise that God intended mankind to live in communion with Him in a beautiful, harmonious environment – the only proviso being that we human beings should be lovingly obedient to Him, just as a human family can be harmonious where there are loving parents and the children are obedient to their parents' wise precepts.

We observe that there are physical laws governing the created world; it is clear, from observing any human society, that there must also be moral laws which are obeyed, if that society is to be healthy.

Chapter 2 of Genesis gives us a detailed account of the separate creation of man and woman. It reads:

Then the Lord God formed man from the dust of the ground and breathed into his nostrils the breath of life; and man became a living being. (v.7)

A little while later:

The Lord God caused the man to fall into a deep sleep; and while he was sleeping He took one of the man's ribs, and closed up the place with flesh. Then the Lord God made a woman from the rib He had taken out of the man, and He brought her to the man. The man said, "This is now bone of my bones, and flesh of my flesh; she shall be called 'woman', for she was taken out of man". (v. 21-23)

The uniqueness of man and his special relationship with God are mentioned briefly in Genesis Chapter 1, in the words:

So God created man in His own image, in the image of God He created him; male and female He created them. And He blessed them. (v. 27-28)

Man and his female counterpart, woman, walked with God and communicated deeply with Him in the Garden of Eden, and all was perfect for them and very good.

It is important, however, to understand that God created man with two qualities that were distinctive from the rest of creation. Firstly, because man is created in the image of God – that is, with a spiritual dimension to his nature – he is capable of a relationship of fellowship and communication with God which no other creature can attain. Secondly, Genesis Chapters 2 and 3 reveal that man was given a free will, either to obey or disobey the requirements of his creator.

And the Lord God commanded the man: "You are free to eat from any tree of the garden; but you must not eat from the tree of the knowledge of good and evil, for when you eat of it you will surely die." (Gen. 2 v 16-17)

When God created man, therefore, He did not create, as we do today, a pre-programmed robot. We can assume that He could, in fact, have done so; but then its obedience to Him would have had no value at all and, as

4

far as we can understand, He could have had no real fellowship with such an object. A robot such as this would not have been created "in the image of God", and would not have achieved God's purpose, which was to have a free, flowing fellowship of love with a spiritual yet physical being.

However, in creating a free being, God sacrificed a large portion of His sovereign rule, because it was intrinsically possible for man to disobey, and rebel against Him. According to the third chapter of Genesis, this is in fact exactly what happened. The man and the woman ate the forbidden fruit and immediately lost their communion with God.

But the Lord God called to the man, "Where are you?"
The 'Fall of Man' immediately brought about three terrible results. The first was the advent of pain, the first mention of which is here in the Bible:

To the woman He said, "I will greatly increase your pains in childbearing; with pain you will give birth to children."

(Gen. 3 v 16)

The second result of the Fall was the cursing of God's beautiful creation:

"Cursed is the ground because of you; through painful toil you will eat of it all the days of your life. It will produce thorns and thistles for you . . . By the sweat of your brow you will eat your food".

(Gen. 3 v 17-19a)

The third consequence of the Fall was the reality of death, with, one may assume, its frequent preceding sickness and pain. God said:

". . .until you return to the ground, since from it you were taken. For dust you are, and to dust you will return."

(Gen. 3 v 19)

5

The Apostle Paul, writing in the first century AD to the church at Rome, takes up this theme:

For the creation was subjected to frustration, not by its own choice, but by the will of the one who subjected it, in hope that the creation itself will be liberated from its bondage to decay. . . We know that the whole creation has been groaning as in the pains of childbirth right up to the present time.

(Romans 8 v 20-22)

Since the Fall therefore, the human body, mind and spirit have been very sensitive to pain, suffering, corruption and death; and the created order, although still retaining much of its beauty, has become almost an alien environment in which man has to live and try to survive, knowing that, however long each individual survives, he or she will one day die.

We now see that the first sentence of this chapter: "This world is not as God intended it to be" summarises the fact that it has been ruined by the Fall of man.

Before we can proceed to examine what God has done to remedy this tragic situation we must look at another very important factor which contributed to man's downfall and which causes much of his suffering and pain. That is the reality of a spiritual being, named variously in the Bible as Lucifer (Isaiah 14 v 12), Satan (Job 1; Matt. 4 v 10 etc), the devil (Matt. 4 v 1-11) and even Beelzebub (Matt. 12 v 24-27), because, according to Genesis Chapter Three, in order for man to fall, he had first to be tempted.

It is obvious, from the Bible, that before God created man to live on earth, He also created other orders of spiritual beings to inhabit the heavenly realms (Colossians 1 v 16). These are referred to as 'angels' and 'archangels', such as Gabriel (Luke 1 v 26) and Michael (Daniel 12 v 1). It seems that Lucifer was also created as an archangel and once took his place as a high-ranking heavenly prince in the order of God's providence. However, in what theologians term a 'pre-cosmic fall', Lucifer, who also had a free will, fell from grace:

> *How you have fallen from heaven*
> *O morning star, son of the dawn!*
> *You have been cast down to the earth,*
> *You who once laid low the nations!*
> *You said in your heart,*
> *"I will ascend to heaven;*
> *I will raise my throne above the stars of God;*
> *. . . I will make myself like the Most High".*
> *But you are brought down to the grave,*
> *to the depths of the pit.*
>
> (Isaiah 14 v 12-15)

and

> *You were the model of perfection*
> *Full of wisdom and perfect in beauty.*
> *You were in Eden, the garden of God;*
> *. . . You were anointed as a guardian cherub,*
> *for so I ordained you.*
> *You were on the holy mount of God . . .*
> *You were blameless in your ways*
> *From the day you were created,*
> *Till wickedness was found in you*
> *. . . and you sinned.*
> *So I drove you in disgrace*
> *From the mount of God. . . .*
> *Your heart became proud*
> *on account of your beauty,*
> *And you corrupted your wisdom*
> *Because of your splendour.*
> *So I threw you to the earth..*
>
> (Ezekiel 28 v 12b-17)

7

Jesus Himself once said that He saw Satan "fall as lightning from heaven" (Luke 10 v 18). It was, apparently, this heavenly princeling who "possessed" the snake in the garden of Eden, and tempted Eve and Adam.

Satan, however, did not fall alone. Many angels also sinned and left their habitation (2 Peter 2 v 4). It is obvious from Scripture that Satan has established a spiritual kingdom to rival and even fight against the Kingdom of God (Rev 12 v 4, 7-8) and his kingdom includes 'principalities' and 'powers' (Ephesians 6 v 12; Colossians 1 v 16) and his lower angels, which are called 'demons' in the gospels, can even "rule" over the human soul and body, causing all manner of emotional and physical sickness and disabilities such as insanity (Mark 5 v 1-20) blindness (Matt. 12 v 22) dumbness (Matt. 9 v 33) epilepsy (Matt. 17 v 14-18) and even severe pain and disability in the spine (Luke 13 v 16). In Job (Chapters 1 and 2) we see that Satan has power to cause murder (Job 1 v 15) fire from heaven (v 16) tornados (v 19) and terrible pain and sickness (2 v 7).

We can see from all this, the fall of Lucifer and the Fall of man, that God's loving, caring, perfect will for the heavens and the earth has been seriously compromised. But this does not mean that He has abdicated His throne. He permits, although I believe with heart-broken grief, the suffering caused by the precious freedom He has given His created beings. This includes wars, murders and all the rest of our human misery which Satan and we bring upon ourselves through our fallen natures. He also permits all the suffering of sickness and the grief engendered by death brought about through His fallen creation. To interfere with our freedom would be to re-create man as a robot. This would be a denial of His nature of love, which desires our love in response.

His **perfect** will is our **perfect** health, life and happiness, but in this present 'dispensation', as theologians call the era in which we live, this is compromised. However, the Bible teaches that one day His perfect will once again will be done on earth as it is in heaven, as He taught us to pray in the 'Lord's Prayer'. It will be done freely by a redeemed humanity when the "kingdom of the world has become the kingdom of our Lord and of His Christ, and He will reign for ever and ever" (Revelation 11 v 15). We see the result of this foretold by the writer of those words, St John the Divine:

Then I saw a new heaven and a new earth; for the first heaven and the first earth had passed away and there was no longer any sea.

I saw the Holy City, the new Jerusalem, coming down out of heaven from God, prepared as a bride beautifully dressed for her husband.

And I heard a loud voice from the throne saying, "Now the dwelling of God is with men, and He will live with them. They will be His people and God Himself will be with them and be their God.

"He will wipe every tear from their eyes. There will be no more death or mourning or crying or pain, for the old order of things has passed away."

He who was seated on the throne said, "I am making everything new . . ." (Revelation 21 v 1-5).

So God's perfect will, in the end, will come to pass. We, in fact, live in the interim period, between the Fall of man and the second coming of Christ, when He will perfectly re-establish His kingdom. At the present time God's sovereignty is still exercised as He

works all things [including sickness, pain and death] *together for the good of those who love Him, who have been called according to His purpose* (Romans 8 v 28).

He has also, as we shall see, declared His will and made it possible for us to attain rewards, total healing, even now – in this world, until through death He calls us home to glory.

Chapter 2
God's will and our wholeness

I believe with all my heart that it is God's perfect will that we should be whole in body, mind and spirit even whilst we are travelling through this world to our ultimate perfect, heavenly state in realms beyond this mortal life. It is obvious, however, from our experience of two thousand years of Christian history, and indeed, from the Bible itself, that Christians are not immune from the suffering caused by the Fall of man and the very imperfect state of the creation. Even the great Apostle Paul, who was used in so much healing ministry, had to write of two of his dearest friends:

Epaphroditus was ill, and almost died. But God had mercy on him (Philippians 2: 27)

and

I left Trophimus sick in Miletus (2 Timothy 4: 20)

and he had to urge Timothy to

use a little wine because of your stomach and your frequent illnesses(1 Tim. 5: 23).

I myself, though wonderfully healed by God of very serious illnesses when I became a Christian at the age of nineteen, have not been free of ailments, both physical and emotional, during my spiritual pilgrimage and life of service to the Lord. However, as I have stated, and proved in my own experience, such infirmities are not God's perfect will for His children, even though He is able to work them together especially for our spiritual maturity and growth.

God disclosed His perfect will towards sickness early in the Bible when He revealed Himself to Moses as "Jehovah Rapha", which is translated into English: "I, the Lord, am your Healer" (Exodus 15: 26).

11

However, the Hebrew means even more than this. Jehovah (or Yahweh) is the very Name of God which can be translated as "I AM WHO I AM" (Exodus 3: 14) and "Rapha" means "Healer". What God was saying to Moses was that His very Nature, His Essence, His very Being, **is Healing**. He is therefore a God of health and wholeness in Himself. It follows that all who seek to bring healing and wholeness to human beings, and even animals, are flowing with the Being, the Will and the purposes of God. This is further expressed by David in a psalm where he sings about the Lord as One who

> *forgives all my sins*
> *and heals all my diseases;*
> *He redeems my life from the pit*
> *and crowns me with love and compassion.*

(Psalm 103: 3-4)

The full expression of God's perfect will towards suffering humanity is, however, seen in all its fullness in the life and ministry of our Lord Jesus Christ. For us Christians, Jesus was more than a prophet and more than a teacher. He was God Himself, incarnate at a certain time and a certain place in human history. So John says of Jesus:

In the beginning was the Word, and the Word was with God, and the Word was God . . .

The Word became flesh and lived for a while among us. We have seen His glory, the glory as of the one and only [Son], who came from the Father, full of grace and truth.

(John 1: 1, 14)

Paul writes:

He is the image of the invisible God

(Colossians 1: 15)

and:

For in Christ all the fullness of the Deity lives in bodily form, (Col. 2: 9)

and Jesus Himself said to Thomas:

Anyone who has seen me has seen the Father . . . Don't you believe that I am in the Father and that the Father is in me?

(John 14: 9-10).

It follows that all that Jesus says is an utterance from God, and that all He does is the work of God and is flowing with His will.

Now even a cursory reading of the Gospels indicates that Jesus' ministry was addressed to the whole person: body, mind and spirit. When He began His public ministry at a synagogue in Nazareth and preached His first sermon, He declared:

> *"The Spirit of the Lord is upon me*
> *Because He anointed me to preach good news*
> *to the poor.*
> *He has sent me to proclaim freedom*
> *for the prisoners*
> *And recovery of sight for the blind,*
> *To release the oppressed,*
> *To proclaim the year of the Lord's favour."*

(Luke 4: 18-19)

In choosing this passage from Isaiah (Is. 61: 2) He was setting out His programme, the blueprint for His whole ministry.

Jesus' ministry was a fulfilment of what He saw to be His Divine commission. Against the backcloth of His constant proclaiming of the Kingdom of God and call to repentance, He ministered to all who came to Him with sickness, disease and demonic possession (Mark 1: 32-34) and in doing this He was fulfilling the will and purposes of God.

13

It is to be noticed that Jesus healed **all** who came to Him for help. Not to anyone did He say, "It is not my Father's will to heal you". One man actually questioned whether it was in the will of Jesus to heal:

A man with leprosy came to Him, and begged Him on his knees, "If You are willing, You can make me clean."

Filled with compassion, Jesus reached out His hand and touched the man. **"I am willing,"** *He said.* *"Be clean!"* (Mark 1: 40-41).

When later ten lepers came to Jesus for healing, He did not say to one, "It is not God's will to heal you" or to another, "Your sickness is doing you good; you must keep it." He healed them all, even though only one actually returned to express his thanks (Luke 17: 11-19). Here we see the perfect will of God toward our suffering, not based on any forlorn hope or human speculation. Only on one occasion Jesus did not heal all the sick; that was at the Pool of Bethesda. But then, they did not in fact ask Him for healing; all their eyes were on the pool (John 5: 1-9). In His ministry He healed all who asked for this blessing, but did not go looking for ministry. This, as we shall see later, is still an important factor to realise in Divine healing ministry today. It is my belief from Scripture, however, that it is God's perfect will to bring total healing to all who seek it from Him.

Chapter 3
Healing and the early church

We have looked at the ministry of Jesus and found that it was addressed to the whole person. With Him, healing and wholeness were forthcoming from God at all times. However, He died upon the cross, rose again and ascended into heaven. So, we might ask, did God's will in response to our needs cease to be wholeness, and did the possibility of His healing power being available for mankind then cease? A further examination of the Gospels reveals this to be far from the case.

We read early in the narrative of Jesus' ministry that He called twelve men to be His disciples and to be in close fellowship with Him. It is evident that He intended to train them fully in the truths and activities of His Kingdom (Luke 6: 13). It is important that we see the spiritual significance of the number twelve and the reason why the disciples considered it important to make up the number to twelve again after the death of Judas (Acts 1: 21-26). This is because there were, in fact, twelve patriarchs, the sons of Jacob (also known as Israel), who were founders, as it were, of the "old" people of God: the Jews, with their twelve tribes. They were in a special relationship with God through the Old Covenant (or Testament).

Now Jesus was bringing into being a new people of God who would be in a new relationship with God; a New Covenant (Luke 22: 20). He therefore chose, as of old, **twelve** new patriarchs of this Covenant, which would be His special people, His Church (Matt. 16: 18). This new people would eventually be formed not only from the Jewish nation, but from "every nation, tribe, people and language" (Rev. 7: 9) and so twenty-four elders sit around the throne of heaven (Rev. 4: 4).

15

So we must understand that the promises made to the twelve apostles and the commissioning and instructions given to them apply to the whole Church for all time until the Lord returns in glory and the Church Age comes to an end.

Jesus not only taught His disciples ('apostles' Luke 6: 13) the essential truths about His Kingdom. He also sent them out on what we may call 'pilot' missions to perform the essential tasks of His church. It is very significant that

When Jesus had called the Twelve together, He gave them power and authority to drive out all demons and to cure diseases, and He sent them out to preach the kingdom of God and to heal the sick. (Luke 9: 1-2)

Sometime, apparently soon afterwards,

the Lord appointed seventy others and sent them two by two ahead of Him to every town and place where He was about to go. (Luke 10: 1)

His instructions to them were:

"Heal the sick who are there and tell them, 'The kingdom of God is near you'." (Luke !0: 9)

Once again we see that this is a "Full Gospel ministry" to the whole person. They were to continue the essential work of Jesus Himself.

It is important to discern several factors which were (and, I would insist, still are) essential ingredients for the work of this embryo church.

Firstly, Jesus gave them **power** (*Greek:* dunamis) – spiritual energy power, a sort of Divine supernatural energy power, without which they would experience no success in their work. No healing could be achieved by purely human effort and energy, no matter how sincerely they were exercised.

16

Secondly, Jesus gave them **authority** (*Greek:* exousia). To complement the dunamis, or supernatural energy power, Jesus delegated to them at least a measure of His own authority as Messiah, Son of Man, and Son of God. It was in fact the authority with which Jesus spoke and ministered, which not only drew crowds of people to Him but brought cries of astonishment from their lips (see Mark 1: 22,27). We should remind ourselves that 'authority' is the power which a person exercises by virtue of his or her status (*cf* the president of the USA). Jesus had incredible authority over even the winds and the waves (Mark 4); and authority can actually be delegated to others who in fact have of themselves only an ordinary status. Jesus delegated His authority, it seems, mainly by giving to ordinary men the right to use **His Name**.

These apostles combated demons and sickness with success whenever they issued their commands in the Name of Jesus because they had been given authority to use His Name, because they were under His authority and because they were on His errands, obeying His commands. The use of this Name guaranteed, as it were, the presence and the authority of the Supreme Person whose name they used. And so:

*The seventy returned with joy, and said, "Lord, even the demons submit to us **in your name**."* (Luke 10: 17)

Another very important fact to realise is that the dealings of Jesus and the apostles with the sick and needy constituted a ministry to them **in their presence** and not prayer for them in their absence. In days of rudimentary transport, they carried, if necessary, the sick to Jesus for His direct ministry to them. This was so, even if to do so meant breaking a hole in the roof of a house (Luke 5: 19). For the sick to be presented in person was, it seems, the normal, right and usual way in which to seek healing or deliverance from demons, from Jesus or the apostles. This was the ministry of the early church to the whole person, again as they, with this ministry, constantly proclaimed the Gospel of the Kingdom of God and called on their hearers to repent and enter into the Divine rule of God in their hearts and lives.

So we move through the Gospel narrative to the evening of the Last Supper, the time when Jesus was giving His farewell discourse to His disciples, praying for their unity and promising them that He would send the Holy Spirit upon them from heaven (John Chapters 13-17). At this point surely the apostles must have been thinking that because Jesus was leaving them and going back to the Father, all the mighty and dramatic deeds of the Kingdom would come to an end; the sick, for instance, would be healed no more. However, Jesus put a stop to any such speculation by uttering some of the most amazing words that ever came from His lips. He said:

"I tell you the truth, anyone who has faith in me will do what I have been doing. He will do even greater things than these, because I am going to the Father.

"And I will do whatever you ask in my name, so that the Son may bring glory to the Father.

"You may ask me for anything in my name, and I will do it."

(John 14 v 12-14)

In other words, Jesus said that after His departure even more would happen through the ministries of those who believed in Him, because He would be in the intimate Presence of the Father. The ministry to the whole person was to continue with even greater effect than ever before, presumably for as long as there were on earth those who believed in Him; that is, for all time until the Lord's return, when it will no longer be needed.

When we turn to the Acts of the Apostles we see what the early Church conceived as its commission from Jesus and how this should be fulfilled. The story begins with the promise given by the risen Jesus that His people would be baptised in the Holy Spirit, and through this immersion of their lives in the Spirit would receive power (dunamis) from on high (Acts 1: 5-8).

Without this infilling of spiritual power, it seems, they could not even begin their God-appointed task. It was on the Day of Pentecost that, as they waited upon God, the promise of Jesus was fulfilled in a mighty outpouring upon the disciples which came in the form of wind and fire and, without doubt, brought them a supernatural endowment which was manifested by their speaking in 'tongues' which they had never learned (Acts 2:1-10).

Having received this wonderful endowment the apostles began their ministry, and we see immediately that it was a full Gospel mission to the whole person. Peter preached with power to assembled crowds, and his message was all about the good news of Jesus. Listeners were "cut to the heart", repented, and believed. Peter told them that the promise of the reception of the power of the Holy Spirit was

for you and your children and for all who are far off (Acts 2: 39).

The promise was for the Church for all generations. So we see Peter preaching the Gospel of the Kingdom of God and thereby bringing salvation to the spiritual lives of those who responded to his call to repent.

However, in Acts Chapter 3 we see Peter and John bringing healing to the body of a man who had been lame from birth. In this account, written by Luke, we see the power and authority with which they exercised their ministry to him. With a word of command Peter said:

"Silver or gold I do not have, but what I have I give you. In the name of Jesus Christ of Nazareth, walk." (Acts 3: 6)

As the man was healed and was "walking and jumping and praising God", Peter said to the astonished crowd:

"By faith in the name of Jesus, this man whom you see and know was made strong. It is Jesus' name and the faith that comes through Him that has given this complete healing to him, as you can all see."

(Acts 3: 16)

This full gospel message and ministry is seen also in the ministry of Philip in Samaria. He

proclaimed the Christ there. (Acts 8: 5)

When the crowds heard Philip and saw the miraculous signs he did, they all paid close attention to what he said. With shrieks, evil spirits came out of many, and many paralytics and cripples were healed. (Acts 8: 6-7)

Acts also records that:

Crowds gathered also from the towns around Jerusalem bringing their sick and those tormented by evil spirits, and all of them were healed. (Acts 5: 16)

Later, Paul also engaged in a full gospel ministry, teaching and preaching the Gospel of Jesus and frequently healing the sick in body and mind (Acts 14: 8-10; 28: 8-9). This was without doubt the ministry of the early Church, wherein they saw themselves fulfilling the commission given to them by Jesus, their Lord.

The Epistles (Letters) of the New Testament also record the beliefs of the early church, and some passages are especially significant in our examination of how the Gospel was conceived to be for the whole person. Paul, for instance, states categorically in his first letter to the Corinthians that there should be, in the church

the effecting of miracles and gifts of healing . . .

(1 Corinthians 12: 9-10, 28), for these, he states, are the work of the Holy Spirit in and through members of the church. He apparently expected sickness and early death to be at least unusual in the Church of God, for he wrote about a wrong attitude to Holy Communion as the cause of such problems amongst the Christians at Corinth:

That is why many among you are weak and sick, and a number of you have fallen asleep. (1 Cor. 11: 30)

Another apostle, James, writes:

Is any one of you sick? He should call the elders of the church to pray over him and anoint him with oil in the name of the Lord. And the prayer offered in faith will make the sick person well; the Lord will raise him up. If he has sinned, he will be forgiven. (James 5: 14-15)

Here it is envisaged that a Christian is sick at home, and he is not enjoined to send a message to the church asking for prayer in his absence. He has to send for the church, in the form of its leaders, the elders, to come to him and minister to him directly; and once again the result, James states, will be wholeness of body and spirit.

There is some conjecture amongst Christians today surrounding another statement about the healing of the whole person as it appears, not in the Epistle of James, but in the first letter of Peter. He writes of Jesus:

He Himself bore our sins in His body on the tree, so that we might die to sins and live for righteousness; **by His wounds you have been healed.** (1 Peter 2: 24.) Here he is quoting directly from the prophecy of Isaiah (Chapter 53: 7) about the death of Jesus. The question is: did Jesus, on the cross, effect the healing of our bodies and minds in the same way as He gained the salvation of our souls?

21

To determine the answer to this question we must realise that Jesus, by bearing the punishment for our sins and making it possible for us to be treated as righteous by God, did not, in fact, perform an act that would make us actually sinless in our Christian lives. In the same manner He did not, to my mind, perform an act that would make it impossible for us to be sick if we put our faith in His shed blood and sacrifice. However, all the blessings we receive from God today, including our reaching out for total healing, derive from His atoning work on Calvary. In the words of the Church of England 1662 Prayer Book, there are "innumerable benefits which by His precious bloodshedding He has obtained for us", and, in my thinking, the possibility of our being healed in body and mind as well as in spirit is included in these. In all the apostles' healing ministry in Acts on not one occasion is a sufferer bidden to put his or her trust in Jesus' atoning work on the Cross; yet, theologically speaking, in the present dispensation, I believe such healing would be impossible without it. I believe that on the cross, and through the ensuing work of the Holy Spirit, and in His Name, Jesus made it possible for us to be totally healed, in body, mind and spirit until He takes us to heaven or returns in glory. As Paul wrote in his first letter to the Thessalonians:

Now may the God of peace Himself sanctify you entirely and may your spirit, soul and body be preserved complete [whole], *without blame at the coming of our Lord Jesus Christ.*

Faithful is He who calls you, and He also will bring it to pass.

(1 Thess. 5: 23-24 *NASV*)

This is God's perfect will for us.

22

PART TWO

The Sacramental Principle

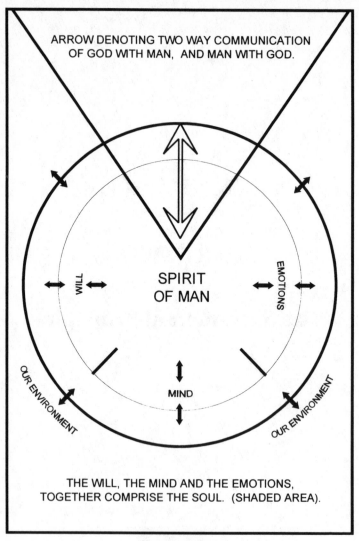

DIAGRAM A

Chapter 4
The nature of man

When we are considering the ways in which God moves to heal us it is important, firstly, to take a look at the nature of a human being as it is conceived to be in the Bible. To help us to do this I have drawn a simple diagram (opposite).

We see from the diagram that, in Biblical teaching, every human being is a trinity of body, soul and spirit (1 Thess. 5: 23). In the very "heart", the innermost being, of a person, is his spirit, through which he has a deep, reciprocal communion with God and through which God's Spirit reaches us. Theologians term this a **mystical** communion which is very difficult, if not impossible, to put into words. As we move outwardly, as it were, we come to the area of the soul. This is made up of our will, our emotions and our thinking capacity which I have called our mind. Beyond this is our body with its five senses: hearing, touching, taste, seeing and smelling, through which we have, again, a reciprocal relationship, this time with all the physical world around us which we call our environment. All of these, spirit, soul and body, make up our total being in the world.

To understand the ways in which God heals us we must realise that, for anything to be real to us, then it must come through one or more of our senses. It was for this reason that God, who is, in Himself, an intangible Spirit, became man and made Himself available to our senses. As John says in his first letter:

That which was from the beginning, which we have heard, which we have seen with our eyes, which we have looked at and our hands have touched – this we proclaim concerning the Word of life. (1 John 1: 1).

25

When He heals us, as we shall see, God also today uses the gateway of our senses.

However, it is important also to realise, as we study the nature of man, that each part – body, soul and spirit – interacts upon the other. So, for example, if we saw (with our body) a bull heading rapidly towards us in a field, we would feel fear in our emotions, giving rise to changes in our body (a rapid heartbeat), in turn reacting on our will and urging us to run.

In the realm of the relationship of our spirit and our emotions, it is noticeable that if we feel depressed in our spirit, then it will affect our relationship with God. Again, if we sin in our spirit it will, if unconfessed, cause a blockage in our communication with God, and cause us to feel "low" in our emotions, perhaps give rise to doubt in our minds, and may even make us feel unwell in our bodies. So we see that all our different parts interact upon each other and all are affected to some degree by our relationship with our environment.

When we consider our total health, even before we examine the ways in which God comes to us to heal us, we must have a right relationship with our environment. As we have seen, since the Fall of man, our environment is rarely ideal and many people are   unhappy with the world around them, including some human relationships in which they are living. Adverse circumstances can, in fact, cause stress, which affects the emotions and even one's relationship with God. It is important that we trust God in such situations and believe that He is "able to work **all things** together for good to those who love Him, who are called according to His purpose" (Romans 8: 28).

We must, in the words of the common adage, learn to accept the things we cannot change (and surrender the situation of our lives to God in a positive way), have courage to change the things we can, and ask God to give us wisdom to know the difference. We must "abandon ourselves to Divine providence" and accept that each moment of our lives is at least permitted by God but can be used, if we react negatively, as material for self-pity, resentment and bitterness. However, if we react positively, even to adverse circumstances, then we can trust the words of St Paul, who went through a great many cruel and savagely distressing experiences in his life and ministry:

we also rejoice in our tribulations, because we know that tribulation produces perseverance; perseverance, character; and character, hope. And hope does not disappoint us, because God has poured out His love into our hearts by the Holy Spirit, whom He has given us. (Romans 5: 3-4)

Paul also urges that we should rejoice in hope and "be patient in affliction" (Rom. 12: 12) and states that, if we trust God, He "comforts us in all our troubles" (2 Corinthians 1: 4).

Because God has made us as spiritual, psychosomatic beings, He actually uses material (including human material) in our environment, such as Christian ministers, to come to us with healing. He uses the senses of our bodies in order to bring about a flowing of His Spirit into the spirit of man. So He uses the **touch** of water in our baptism; the **taste** of bread and wine in Holy Communion; the **hearing** of the Word in preaching, and the sense of **touch** in the laying on of hands and anointing with oil. This I have called the sacramental principle. All the above can be vehicles of healing which God will use to heal our fallen spirits, souls and bodies when they are sick. In healing in particular, however, according to the Bible God uses the sense of touch when the laying on of hands and anointing of the **head** with oil represents the whole

person; every area of the body, mind and spirit
(James 5: 16).

This use of touch was especially important in the
ministry of our Lord Jesus Christ. When Jesus healed a
leper we read:

*Jesus reached out His hand and **touched** the man.*

(Matt. 8: 30)

When He healed Peter's mother-in-law of a fever

*He **touched** her hand and the fever left her,*

(Matt. 8: 15).

When He healed the blind men:

*Then He **touched** their eyes . . . and their sight was
restored.* (Matt. 9: 29-30)

On the mount of transfiguration:

*But Jesus came and **touched** them. "Get up," He said.
"Don't be afraid."* (Matt. 17: 7)

Again, of the blind:

*Jesus had compassion on them and **touched** their eyes.
Immediately they received their sight* (Matt. 20: 34).

Of a deaf-mute:

*After He took him aside, away from the crowd, Jesus put
His fingers into the man's ears . . . and **touched** the man's
tongue . . . the man's ears were opened, his tongue was loosened
and he began to speak plainly.* (Mark 7: 33-35)

In Nazareth:

He laid His hands on a few sick people and healed them
(Mark 6: 5).

Luke records:

*When the sun was setting, the people brought to Jesus all
who had various kinds of sickness, and laying His hands on each
one, He healed them.* (Luke 4: 40)

In Mark's Gospel Jesus further promised that those
who believe in Him

"will place their hands on sick people, and they will get well." (Mark 16: 18)

In my own personal ministry I have laid hands on thousands of people, and seen many of them healed. I have not, however, felt any power, like electricity, flowing through my arms and hands, and I do not feel that this is to be conceived as how God works. I am persuaded that there is nothing "magical" about "healing hands". The sense of touch, I believe, is to be involved so that God, according to His promise, will move through a sufferer's spirit, through their soul and reach the need where it is in their mind or body, as shown in the diagram. When a perfect connection is made between God's Spirit and man's spirit, soul and body, then I believe that no limit can be set on the healing that will take place, for

"nothing is impossible with God" (Luke 1: 37).

I am persuaded, however, that not only the sense of touch but also the spoken word are vitally important in healing ministry; and to this we will now turn.

Chapter 5
The powerful word

We all know and experience the power of human words, whether spoken or written. The words we utter have a power within them either to bless and edify the hearer, or conversely to hurt, damage and destroy. Many of us have, perhaps, during our lifetime either spoken or written words to others that, on reflection, we wish we could withdraw. However, even if we express our regret to those we have hurt, the damage is hard to undo, and often the words still live on, doing their destructive work. As Christians we should indeed ask the Lord, as David did, to set a watch over our lips (see Psalm 141: 3) and hearken to James' advice in his letter, about the power of the tongue (James 1: 26; Chapter 3). Also, perhaps many of us are still suffering from harsh and barbed words spoken to us by such people as parents, teachers, so-called friends, or even pastors. Let us always seek to edify and encourage others by our words, for they have even more power to bless than they have to hurt.

If the power of human words can be so great, how much more power indeed have the words which God speaks, either in general to the human race (*Greek* logos) or directly to an individual (*Greek* rhema); for as Christians we believe not only in a God who has spoken in the past in the Bible and especially in Jesus, but also in a God who speaks to us today.

The Bible itself speaks about the **power** of God's words. So it teaches that He actually spoke this universe into existence and it was a word from Him which set the sun ablaze. The first chapter of the book Genesis, which describes creation, continually says: "God said . . ." (for instance: "'Let there be light', and there was light" – Gen. 1: 2). Peter also says:

by the word of the Lord were the heavens made.

(2 Pet. 3: 5)

and the writer of the letter to the Hebrews says that Jesus *sustains all things by His powerful word.*

(Hebrews 1: 3)

In other words, if God stopped speaking, everything would fall into chaos and even cease to exist. So we can set no limits whatsoever on the power of God's Word to achieve what He desires.

Further to the Bible's teaching about the power of God's words, we also see that it teaches about the **permanence** of His utterances. Isaiah expresses this truth when he says:

The grass withers and the flowers fall,
but the word of our God stands for ever.

(Isaiah 40: 8)

and

so is My word that goes out from My mouth:
It will not return to Me empty,
but will accomplish what I desire
and achieve the purpose for which I sent it.

(Isaiah 55: 11)

Jesus Himself also said:

"Heaven and earth will pass away, but my words will never pass away." (Matt. 24: 35)

In the Bible another very important statement on this theme is about the **penetration** of God's word. The writer to the Hebrews states:

The word of God is living and active. Sharper than any double-edged sword, it penetrates even to dividing soul and spirit, joints and marrow; (Hebrews 4: 12).

This text indicates that once the word of God has, as it is able to do, reached the very depths of our being, then it is alive and active within us, doing God's work in our spirits,

souls and bodies. So, for instance, if we swallow a
medication prescribed by our doctor, it usually contains a
chemical substance within it which becomes active in our
bodies and can even affect our minds and emotions. How
much more powerful then is the living and active word of
God when it is at work within us!

Finally, in our consideration of the Word of God, we
see that the Bible teaches about the **purpose** of God's
Word. This, in fact, is always for our good and especially
for bringing about our wholeness and healing. In the Old
Testament, for example, the psalmist says of God:

He sent forth His word and healed them;

(Psalm 107: 20).

However, it is especially on the lips of Jesus that we see
the power, permanence, penetration and purpose of God's
word:

He **spoke** to a storm and there was a great calm.
(Mark 4: 39)

He **spoke** and Lazarus came back to life.
(John 11: 43)

He said:

*"I tell you the truth, a time is coming and has now come
when the dead will hear the voice of the Son of God and those
who hear will live."*

(John 5: 25)

Jesus did not only lay hands on sick people; He **spoke**
healing to them and they were restored. In the case of
Peter's mother-in-law Luke records:

He rebuked the fever, and it left her. (Luke 4: 39)

To a leper He said:

"I am willing. Be clean!" *Immediately the leprosy left
him and he was cured.* (Mark 1: 41-42)

To a man with a withered hand:

"Stretch out your hand." . . . *and his hand was completely restored.* (Mark 3: 5)

To a blind man:

"Go, your faith has healed you." *Immediately he received his sight and followed Jesus along the road.* (Mark 10: 52)

Sometimes the word of healing was mixed with a word which brought forgiveness:

He said "Friend, your sins are forgiven." (Luke 5: 20)

"But so that you may know that the Son of Man has authority on earth to forgive sins . . ." *He said to the paralysed man, "I tell you, get up, take your mat and go home."* *Immediately he stood up in front of them.* (Luke 5: 24-25)

Jesus also **spoke** deliverance to those who were demonised:

And Jesus rebuked him saying, "Be quiet and come out of him" . . .*and the unclean spirit came out of him.* (Mark 1: 25)

and of the Gadarene demoniac it is recorded that Jesus

was saying to him, "Come out of this man, you evil spirit!"

(Mark 5: 8)

In all this we see the healing power of God's spoken word.

We must, however, note in passing, that in order to make us whole, sometimes God has had to speak a penetrating and "hard" word to His people as He did to Israel through the prophets of the Old Testament, and as Jesus did to the Pharisees in the New. This hard word, however disturbing it may have been, was always for man's ultimate restoration and well-being.

God still speaks today for our healing, and this is frequently a 'rhema' word to our hearts.

He speaks through promises in the Bible which we can appropriate as promises to our own hearts.

He speaks through preachers who are faithful to the Gospel message of the Bible as they apply it to our lives.

He speaks through gifts of the Holy Spirit on the mouths of inspired men and women. This can be through a prophecy or word of knowledge (1 Cor. 12) which actually describes our need in detail and promises God's healing.

He speaks through the circumstances and situations of our lives when we are given discernment in them to hear what He is saying to us.

He speaks through visions and dreams, as He did in situations recorded in the Bible.

He speaks through counsellors, Christian friends, and through seemingly chance words which are spoken to us.

He speaks to us directly in our innermost beings, often in periods of prayer, meditation, silence or stillness.

Jesus promised that, in His role as the Good Shepherd, His sheep would both hear and recognise His voice (John 10: 1-18), amongst and distinct from the many voices which would call for their attention. We can learn to do this by studying the way God speaks in the Bible, recognising that He will never contradict that word, and testing whether or not we have really heard God's word by consulting mature, Spirit-filled Christian leaders.

There can be no doubt that God has used His written and spoken word in the past and is still doing so today to penetrate and bring about a flow of His healing, life-giving Spirit within our innermost beings, flooding, in turn, immediately or gradually, our souls and bodies to bring them towards total wholeness.

Chapter 6
Faith

A sacrament is an outward and visible sign of an inward and spiritual grace, and there are two major sacraments recognised by all Christians; the use of water in baptism and bread and wine in Holy Communion. Through these physical and tangible means, God, we believe, moves with His Spirit into the realm of the human spirit (see diagram A, p.24) and brings His blessing to the whole person. We have seen, however, that He also uses the sense of touch in the laying on of hands, the sense of hearing through His spoken word, and the sense of sight through His written word, to move in our lives to bring about the healing of the whole person.

In the Bible it is recorded also that He used water for the healing of Naaman the leper (2 Kings Chapter 5). There was also the use of saliva and clay by Jesus to heal a blind man (John 9: 6) and even aprons and handkerchiefs (Acts 19: 12) to bring healing and deliverance to the afflicted. However, we must appreciate that none of these outward means were magical in the blessings they produced. The grace of God in all its many operations had to be appropriated by faith on the part of the seeker.

It was especially in the receipt of healing that our Lord Jesus Christ commended sick people for their faith. To a centurion He said:

> *"I have not found anyone in Israel with such great faith."*
> (Matt. 8: 10)

To those bringing a paralysed man for healing:

> When Jesus **saw their faith**, He said to the paralytic, *"Take heart, son; your sins are forgiven."* (Matt. 9: 2)

To a woman healed of a haemorrhage:

> *"your faith has healed you."* (Matt. 9: 22)

To two blind men:
> *"According to your faith will it be done to you."*
>
> (Matt. 9: 29)

To a leper:
> *"Rise and go; your faith has made you well."*
>
> (Luke 17: 19)

and to another blind man:
> *"Receive your sight; your faith has healed you."*
>
> (Luke 18: 42)

What then is the nature of this faith which is so important if we are to receive God's healing power into our whole being? To answer this question we can do no better than to look at the teaching of Jesus Himself on this subject. In Mark (Chapter 11: 22-24), after the cursing of a fig tree, Jesus said to His disciples:

> *"Have faith in God,*
>
> *"I tell you the truth, if anyone says to this mountain, 'Go, throw yourself into the sea,' and does not doubt in his heart but believes that what he says will happen, it will be done for him.*
>
> *"Therefore I tell you, whatever you ask for in prayer, believe that you have received it, and it will be yours."*

I see in Jesus' teaching four necessary ingredients of faith: awareness; expectancy; assurance and , finally, action. We shall study these one at a time.

Firstly, then, **awareness**:

When Jesus chose a mountain to illustrate what is possible for God to do in response to faith, He chose in fact the most immovable object on earth. We may climb over mountains, go around them or even tunnel through them, but we cannot move them because they are part of the earth's crust. What Jesus was, in fact, saying can be put in these words:

"Do not set any barriers around what God can do in answer to faithful prayer!" "Do not think: this is a small request therefore it is possible, but that particular desire is too great a thing for God to accomplish."

Now, we must see that there is a great deal of difference between **belief** that God can do anything we ask, and an **awareness** that He can do so. Before I was baptised in the Holy Spirit and launched into a healing ministry I regularly recited the creed which contains the words:

"I believe in God the Father **almighty**."

If anyone had asked me if I believed anything to be impossible for God to do, I would have uttered a definite "No!" However, when I saw a woman at a Pentecostal church, after ministry by a pastor, rise in the Name of Jesus and walk, having been paralysed for fourteen years, I became **aware** of what God could do.

Similarly, in the Rite A Holy Communion Service in the Church of England, the priest says at one stage:

"The Lord is here."

And the people respond:

"His Spirit is with us."

When these words are uttered I believe they are usually stating a definite belief about the Presence of the Lord in the Service. But are the majority really **aware** of Jesus' presence and of all that can be accomplished in that meeting of God's people because He is really there?

So, as we minister to even the desperately sick and crippled and as they receive ministry, both the minister and the recipient of ministry, and, I believe, everyone present, should be **aware** that nothing is impossible with God.

Next, we turn to the ingredient of **expectancy**:

Jesus, I believe, is saying about faith in God:

"Be aware that what you ask can take place and then expect it to do so." – He said that there should be no doubt in our minds that what we ask for is, in fact, **going to happen**. Do we, when we minister, or receive ministry, or pray for healing, really **expect** that it is going to take place?

How frequently is our expectancy like that of a woman who tried to move a slag heap which was in front of the window of her house and was blocking what would have been a lovely view of a valley!

"Bert," she said to her husband, "I'm going to command this slag heap to move into the North Sea, in the Name of Jesus."

That night, before going to bed, she opened the window, pointed at the slag heap, and commanded it to move. The next morning she drew back the curtains, looked out of the window and exclaimed to her husband:

"Bert, it's still there, *just as I thought*, just as I thought!"

So when someone is not healed the voice of our own minds may be inclined to say, "s/he is – or I am – no better, just as I thought." No! Jesus teaches us that if we truly have faith in God, we will **expect** the mountain of sickness, incapacity, or adverse circumstances really to move.

Awareness and expectancy should pass into an **assurance**

that God has in fact performed the miracle. Jesus said that we should be able to believe that we **have** received that for which we ask God. This means that we are **absolutely certain** that we have in fact received. How this assurance comes about is difficult to ascertain or describe. However, we actually know "within ourselves" that the miracle has taken place. We would, if necessary, give our lives for this fact. I believe that this "inner witness" precedes even any tangible, visible results or even medical verification that a person has been healed, for instance, when we have asked in faith.

Once all these ingredients of our faith are really there, then, and only then, is the time for **action.**

Jesus told us to go and speak to the mountain, and James further teaches that

> *faith by itself, if it is not accompanied by action, is dead.*
>
> (James 2: 17)

– it doesn't really exist!

Once we have become **certain** within ourselves that we have been healed, and only then, is the time, for example, to dispense with our medical aids. To do so in order to see, as it were, whether through a particular ministry God has really worked for us, is an act of doubt, which can lead to disappointment and even disaster. However, a miracle of God's blessing in healing will not take place unless we begin to live in the faith that we are whole and healthy people.

In all this discussion of the ingredients of faith we must understand that Jesus did not say simply "have faith" and blessing will occur. Further, He did not say "have faith in faith" or even "have faith in the minister of healing". He did, in fact, say, "Have faith in God"!

I am sure that faith does not come to us by thinking about it as such, or examining whether or not we have it. It comes by meditating and dwelling upon the Being and Nature of God, of whom Charles Wesley wrote:

> "His love is as great as His power,
> And neither knows measure nor end."

And as Paul said also of faith:

faith comes from hearing the message, and the message is heard through the word of Christ..

(Rom. 10: 17)

It is interesting to note that in the instances of healing cited at the beginning of this chapter, the persons who were healed by Jesus had in fact to be told **by Him** that it was their faith in Him which had made them whole; because, apparently, they weren't even thinking about whether or not they had this particular virtue of faith. They came to Jesus sure that He could, and hoping that He would heal them.

All the truths we have examined are graphically portrayed in the account of the woman who came to Jesus seeking healing from haemorrhage which had made her ill for twelve years (Mark 5: 25-34).

She had an incurable illness which was her "mountain" of sickness;

she had heard about Jesus and His miracle-working power which came from God (here was her **awareness** of what Jesus could do);

she thought she would be healed by touching His cloak (the tangible, physical **"sacrament"** which was available to her sense of touch);

she thought, "If I just touch His garments I **shall** get well" (Here was intense **expectancy**);

"she felt in her body that she was freed from her suffering" (v 29) (Here was **assurance** – she was sure of what had happened to her [v 33]).

Jesus then had to tell her that it was not any "magic" in His cloak, but said:

"Daughter, your faith has healed you."

So we see this faith in action, as we do also in the ministry, not only of Jesus, but of Peter, in the healing of

40

the lame man at the Beautiful Gate of the temple (Acts 3). Peter used the authority of the Name of Jesus after the Lord's ascension, and spoke healing to the lame man. Later he said:

"By **faith in the name of Jesus**, *this man whom you see and know was made strong. It is Jesus' name and the faith that comes through Him that has given this complete healing to him, as you can all see."*   (Acts 3: 16)

Thankfully, if we wilt under this teaching, we can be encouraged by Jesus' words:

"if you have faith as small as a mustard seed, you can say to this mountain, 'Move from here to there' and it will move. Nothing will be impossible for you."

(Matt. 17: 20).

Chapter 7
Healing and the Church today

The ministry of Word and Sacrament which God uses to bring total healing to our spirits, souls and bodies are within the domain of the Christian Church. The Church is the custodian of these means of grace. This ministry of Divine healing, which is in the name of Jesus, for His glory, is an integral part of the Gospel of the Kingdom which the Church proclaims and administers.

It is therefore very important to differentiate it from other forms of "spiritual healing", especially the psychic approach which may, in fact, bring healing to the soul and body, but is not, in fact, addressed to the spirit of man, and may even bring the recipient into satanic bondage. All forms of spirit religion are denounced in the Bible as not coming directly from the true God, and are portrayed as an abomination to Him. God commanded His people not to practise "divination or sorcery" (Leviticus 19: 26) and then says:

"Do not turn to mediums or seek out spiritists, for you will be defiled by them. I am the Lord your God."

Further:

"I will set My face against the person who turns to mediums and spiritists to prostitute himself by following them, and I will cut him off from his people." (Lev. 20: 6)

And again:

"Let no one be found among you . . . who practises divination or sorcery, interprets omens, engages in witchcraft, or casts spells, or who is a medium or spiritist or who consults the dead. Anyone who does these things is detestable to the Lord." (Deuteronomy 18: 10-12)

In 2 Chronicles it is said of King Manasseh that he

consulted mediums and spiritists. He did much evil in the eyes of the Lord, provoking Him to anger (2 Chron. 33:6).

42

Paul, in the New Testament, actually says Satan uses these things as "all kinds of counterfeit miracles, signs and wonders, and in every sort of evil that deceives" (2 Thess. 2: 9-10) and that those who do these things are "false apostles, deceitful workmen, . . . for Satan himself masquerades as an angel of light" (2 Cor. 11: 13-14) and God even measures out drastic punishment for them.

> *"A man or woman who is a medium or spiritist must be put to death. You are to stone them; their blood will be on their own heads."* (Lev 20: 27)

It is very important therefore that we see the true ministry and receipt of total healing as within the Christian Church. However, it was when I first began to challenge pastors at teaching seminars to launch out into Spirit-empowered healing ministry in their various churches that I was soon brought to realise that such men felt very insecure about engaging in this work. Most reacted favourably to suggestions about preaching the gospel because that was what they had generally been trained to do. It was a different matter, however, when I came to the need to lay hands on the sick. Such teaching often met with real hostility.

Frequently, when talking to groups of ministers, I discovered that underlying their objections to this ministry was the fact that they did not know just when, where or how to begin. They felt also that they would inevitably be out on their own, remote from their congregations. So I had to emphasise that healing ministry was the function of the **whole community of believers** as they sought to be made whole together.

Most ministers, of course, are very ready to pray for the sick in their absence, because this has been the accepted procedure in the tradition of most denominations of the Church. As a pastor I had done so myself, nearly every Sunday, even to mentioning the needy people by name. Some ministers, I discovered, had even gone as far as praying in the presence of sick people, when visiting them in their homes. Such prayers had, of course, always included an "if it be Thy will" clause. These words sound pious enough, but they cut at the very root of faith which believes that we are actually receiving what we ask for. They can be simply a way of escape in case nothing happens. Such prayers demand little faith of either church or pastor.

In pastors' gatherings, however, I have refused to accept these practices as a complete ministry to the sick. I have pointed to the example of our Lord, and indeed to the whole New Testament, as showing clearly that the Bible rarely mentions praying for the sick in their absence; it focuses attention on ministering to them **in their presence**. Of course, I have readily acknowledged that God does answer intercessory prayer for the sick – because He is an all powerful, faithful, loving Father. However, that is not the way into supernatural power and the realm of healing miracles. Actually, to minister to the sick, as did Jesus and the early Christians, had proved for me to be the breakthrough into the supernatural dimension in healing. I had seen it to be so in the ministries of scores of others. Ever since, therefore, I have urged it as the way of obedience for every pastor I have met.

The firm line I have taken has definite support from the epistle of James. Addressing sick Christians, apparently too ill to be "in church", the inspired writer urges:

Is any one of you sick? He should call the elders of the church to pray over him and anoint him with oil in the name of the Lord. And the prayer offered in faith will make the sick person well; the Lord will raise him up. If he has sinned, he will be forgiven. Therefore confess your sins to each other and pray for each other so that you may be healed. The fervent prayer of a righteous man is powerful and effective. (James 5: 14-16.)

This passage is very interesting because it teaches:

a) The elders of the church are to minister, as elders. There is no suggestion that they are especially gifted. They are certainly not visiting evangelists on a special healing mission. The fact that James says that the elders are to minister shows that healing ministry is envisaged as part of the supernaturally normal life of the Church.

b) They actually minister to the sick person as Jesus did, using words, hands, and even oil. There is no suggestion that praying for this person in his absence should be the normal procedure. Quite the opposite is true. James urges that when a Christian is sick, he should call for the elders. On receiving this request, their duty is not simply to pray for the sick person at the next church service, but to go and minister directly to his needs.

c) Faith is seen as a very important factor in healing. There is no questioning of God's will. Healing, whether sudden or gradual, is normative and is to be taken for granted. It is the result to be expected. This is in harmony with the teaching of the Lord of the Church about the nature of faith (Mark 11:22-24).

d) The character of the ministers is important. They are to be righteous and also men of faithful, powerful prayer.

e) We see, as in the ministry of our Lord, that forgiveness of sin and the healing of the body are very closely linked. Apparently unconfessed sin, like doubt, is a barrier to healing. Again, we see that the healing of the soul is basic to the health of the body. This is where the emphasis of James's ministry is squarely placed.

45

Confession is good for the soul, for the body, and for the whole person.

This passage shows us, 1 believe, the normal procedure in dealing with sickness in the early church. This was how the early Christians were taught, and, no doubt, this was how they acted. There is not the slightest reason for abandoning this practice today.

This ministry of elders, however, **presupposes the existence of a church which itself is healthy, united, expectant and powerful**. This is because the elders are not using their own gift, but are ministering the endowment which God has bestowed upon the church. Theirs is a representative act, performed on behalf of the whole church to which they belong.

The reason for this is better understood if we turn to Paul's first letter to the church at Corinth. There, as in other places, he teaches that the Church is like a body which has many members or, as we would say, organs (Cor. 12, Rom. 12, Eph. 4). The important factor about parts of our bodies is that they share a common life, energy and health. They are all served by the same bloodstream and are dependent upon each other for their very life. If a part of the body, for instance, a kidney, becomes sick, then the whole body is vitally affected. "If one member suffers, all suffer together"(1 Cor. 12:26).

In fact, from modern medical knowledge, we can go further than Paul, and say here positively, "If one member (organ) is sick, all the healing power of the body rushes to its aid". All the healing resources of the body unite to overcome the threat to its life.

Here we have a picture of the church's (eldership) ministry of healing. A member of the church body becomes sick. Therefore, all the other members: the rest of the church, feel his pain. The whole church is involved. The elders, therefore, are called to lay hands on the sick person. In doing so, they function as the vital organs of the whole body. They are the channels through which the healing power of the body will flow to the sick member. However, the health of the whole body is involved – not just that of the elders themselves. The elders call upon all the church's resources of faith, prayer and love to be behind them in their ministry. If there is disunity, discord and doubt prevalent in the body, the flow of God's healing Spirit will be impeded.

It was a sad fact that the church of Corinth was itself sinfully divided. Paul had to write:

> That is why many among you are weak and sick, and a
> number of you have fallen asleep. (1 Cor. 11:30)

Healing ministry was apparently not effective at Corinth, a church that excelled in supernatural gifts, because they brought their sinful self-love even to the Communion service and did not "recognise the body of the Lord" (v. 29).

Today's healing ministry, unfortunately, can sometimes be caricatured as a congregation coming together like a crowd who have turned up to watch spectacular events. They have no sense of being a body of believers or of having a vital part to play in the ministry. "Let's go to see if it works." "Let's see if the pastor can heal someone this week!" "He's not doing very well – probably because he's out of tune with the Lord" are the unspoken thoughts of many people.

The pastor therefore feels himself to be out on his own. Even if, as he should, he calls the other elders to join him in ministering, they too can begin to feel that, humanly speaking, healing depends entirely upon them. "We have not been able to heal many people," they may conclude. "We had better send for an evangelist to see if he can do better!"

I have often been conscious that this has been the attitude of large parts of the congregation at "Miracle Services". People can so easily have come along to watch some spiritual performer "do his stuff". When I have sensed the prevalence of this attitude, I have stopped ministering and explained to the Christians that we are all involved together in the work. I have called them to earnest, expectant prayer. We have then praised the Lord together for those who are healed.

Very occasionally it may be right that the emphasis is mainly on the gifts of a very special person, but even then that person needs enormous prayer support. These times are, however, exceptions to the general rule. I believe that the Lord's primary purpose today is to restore all over the world the Church's ministry of healing for the good of His people and the extension of His kingdom.

This is so, despite the fact that, throughout history, God has raised up specifically gifted people and focused attention upon them. He has done so also in our time. This has been, however, for the inspiration and encouragement of the whole Church. Christians have totally misunderstood the purposes of God if they see such gifted ministries as superseding or replacing the regular ministries of the Church. The work of especially gifted people, in any sphere of ministry, is not to draw attention to themselves. It is their function to encourage, inspire, teach and further the normal ministry, which should be in progress everywhere because Christ is present in His Church.

In this respect we can draw a parallel between the role of the gifted healer and that of the gifted preacher. It is customary for a sermon to be preached in every Christian church on the Lord's day. The eldership of each local church has an obligation to see that this is so, either by doing so themselves, or by appointing someone else to preach. They do not wait for one of the world's gifted preachers to arrive before someone goes into the pulpit! The Church has a duty to preach regularly! If a gifted preacher arrives, he may well be given prominence and inspire the church – but the local preaching does not depend on such. It goes on all the time!

It is exactly the same with the healing ministry and gifted healers. Every church, everywhere, should minister to the sick as part of its normal church life; when gifted healers arrive, or are recognised within the local church, it is to inspire and encourage the regular healing ministry of that church, and in its life **together**. In fact such gifted ministry will be itself hindered if such spiritual togetherness in love and faith does not exist amongst all the believers.

Eldership is conceived of differently by different denominations, but it is always present, because the church could not function without it. In most denominations the ordained ministers or clergy are the focal point of eldership, but their office is not exclusive. When I was a vicar, my churchwardens ministered with me, as elders. Baptists and other denominations have deacons to take this role. Presbyterians certainly have lay elders. There is no excuse for not getting on with the job.

Special people are, therefore, by no means essential for the healing ministry. Although healing can take place on the spot where the sick person actually is, the normal time and place for such ministries is where the church body regularly meets for worship. I have deliberately stayed in churches where I have been leading a mission in order to minister to the needs of the people during normal Sunday services. Sometimes this has been in the context of a Communion service, during the partaking of the bread and wine; on other occasions it has been during the prayer time in morning or evening worship. Another suitable moment has been during the hymn after the sermon, thus enabling the request for ministry to be in response to the spoken word. In some cases ministry has taken place in a meeting afterwards for which, in my experience, most people have willingly stayed.

I have found that special prayer groups for the sick, perhaps midweek, in a home, hall or vestry, have sometimes been necessary as an intermediary stage in introducing divine healing ministry to a church or area. The aim, however, must eventually be to have the gospel of the healing of the whole person proclaimed by words and deeds when the whole body of believers usually meets for worship, and when they can believe together for healing.

If the ministry is to be seen in its evangelistic as well as its pastoral perspective, it is also important that everyone in the locality is made aware that healing ministry is practised in their local church where Christians believe together for wholeness in body, mind and spirit. It is for this reason that regularity of ministry, at the customary services, is a distinct advantage. We have really "arrived" when divine healing ministry is as normal as receiving Communion or hearing a sermon. Expectancy, however, must always be encouraged.

Like all other aspects of church life, divine healing ministry can be inaugurated or boosted by having a time of special emphasis upon it. This can be a time for inviting a gifted guest minister along to help the local church. Mass leaflet distribution, posters, media coverage and personal testimonies can be brought into play. I have often taken part in such efforts at the invitation of churches, and the results have truly glorified the Lord as we have seen hundreds of people who would normally be considered outsiders converted to Christ.

The fact is that most people search for God to meet the needs of their bodies, minds or circumstances before they even understand the importance of the salvation of their souls. It was mainly physical needs which brought people seeking the help of Christ and the apostles. It is the same today with His Church.

It is important that people are not compelled to become disciples before their physical needs are met. This was never so with Jesus. In the case of the ten lepers, sadly, only one even bothered to come back to give thanks. Similarly, we must minister together today to all who come to us sincerely. However, we also remember that our Lord's ministry to physical needs was always against the background of the proclamation of the kingdom of God. There must, in our day, therefore, be no separation of the healing of the body or mind from the total message of the reign of Christ over the whole human life.

PART THREE

The healing of the spirit

Chapter 8
The healing of the spirit and the cross

Ever since the Fall of man the human spirit has been sick. We are, in fact, every one of us, born spiritually sick, with a condition theologians term 'original sin'. Isaiah said of mankind:

> *Your whole head is injured,*
> *your whole heart afflicted.* (Is. 1: 5)

Jeremiah also affirmed this:

> *The heart is more deceitful than all else*
> *and is desperately sick.*
> *Who can understand it?* (Jer. 17: 9 *NASV*)

However, it is Paul, in his epistles, who paints the most graphic picture of the sinful state of man. In his letter to the Romans he first laments man's failure to acknowledge the greatness of God as evidenced in the created world:

> *For since the creation of the world God's invisible qualities – His eternal power and divine nature – have been clearly seen, being understood from what has been made, so that men are without excuse.* (Rom. 1: 20)

He then declares:

> *For although they knew God, they neither glorified Him as God nor gave thanks to Him, but their thinking became futile and their foolish hearts were darkened. Although they claimed to be wise, they became fools and exchanged the glory of the immortal God for images made to look like mortal man and birds and animals and reptiles.*
>
> *Therefore God gave them over in the sinful desires of their hearts to sexual impurity for the degrading of their bodies with one another.*
>
> *They exchanged the truth of God for a lie, and worshipped and served created things rather than the Creator – who is forever praised. Amen.*

For this reason God gave them over to degrading passions
. . . God gave them over to a depraved mind, to do what
ought not to be done. They have become filled with every kind of
wickedness, evil, greed and depravity.

They are full of envy, murder, strife, deceit and malice.
They are gossips, slanderers, God-haters, insolent, arrogant and
boastful; they invent ways of doing evil; they disobey their
parents; they are senseless, faithless, heartless, ruthless. Although
they know God's righteous decree that those who do such things
deserve death, they not only continue to do these very things but
also approve of those who practise them. (Romans 1: 20-32)

And Paul further teaches, quoting from passages of the
psalms, that this innate sinful condition is common to all
mankind:

> *There is no one righteous, not even one,*
> *there is no one who understands,*
> *no one who seeks God.*
> *All have turned away,*
> *they have together become worthless;*
> *there is no one who does good, not even one.*
> *Their throats are open graves;*
> *their tongues practise deceit.*
> *The poison of vipers is on their lips.*
> *Their mouths are full of cursing and bitterness.*
> *Their feet are swift to shed blood;*
> *ruin and misery mark their ways,*
> *and the way of peace they do not know.*
> *There is no fear of God before their eyes.*
>
> (Romans 3: 10-18)

And:

> *all have sinned and fall short of the glory of God.*
>
> (Rom. 3: 23)

In his letter to the Ephesians Paul further writes of the
natural state of man:

As for you, you were dead in your transgressions and sins, in which you used to live when you followed the ways of this world and of the ruler of the kingdom of the air, the spirit who is now at work in those who are disobedient.

All of us also lived among them at one time, gratifying the cravings of our sinful nature and following its desires and thoughts. Like the rest, we were by nature objects of wrath.

(Ephesians 2: 1-3)

Such is the fallen, naturally sick state of the human spirit and the thoughts and deeds it provokes. However, the whole thrust of the New Testament scriptures is to state that God Himself has acted in His Son, the Messiah, Jesus Christ, to remedy this desperate situation and make it possible for the spirit ("heart") of man to be made totally whole. This is the Gospel, the Good News, of which the Church is the custodian and which it is called upon to proclaim to mankind in every age. Through response to the Gospel message every person born can enter into a new relationship with God, and through this relationship his or her spirit can be made whole.

Mark records that Jesus began His public ministry by coming into Galilee,

proclaiming the good news of God. "The time has come," *He said. "The kingdom of God is near. Repent and believe* [or "put your trust in"] *the gospel!"*

(Mark 1: 14-15)

The whole impetus of His ministry to the spiritual needs of mankind can be summed up in His own words:

"It is not the healthy who need a doctor, but the sick. I have not come to call the righteous, but sinners to repentance."

(Luke 5: 31-32)

Furthermore, there is no doubt that Jesus linked His healing of people's spirits to His approaching death. Well into His ministry He stated:

"For even the Son of Man did not come to be served, but to serve, and to give His life as a ransom for many."

(Mark 10: 45)

On the night before His death, at what we call the "Last Supper", He said:

"Take and eat; this is my body."

Then He took the cup, gave thanks, and offered it to them, saying, "Drink from it, all of you.

"This is my blood of the covenant, which is poured out for many for the forgiveness of sins."

(Matt. 26: 26-28)

After Jesus' death on the cross, His resurrection and ascension, and after receiving the power of the Holy Spirit on the Day of Pentecost, Peter preached the Gospel to crowds of people – and what he said was obviously what the early church felt the essence of the Good News to be:

- Jesus of Nazareth was attested by God through miracles and signs which God performed through Him
- He was predetermined to die on the cross at the hands of sinful men as predicted by the prophets
- God raised Him up again as foretold in the Scriptures
- He has been exalted to the right hand of God
- He has poured out the Holy Spirit
- God has made Him Lord and Christ

(Acts 3: 14-36)

- He will return   (Acts 3: 20-21)
- Therefore all should repent and turn to God so that their sins may be wiped away   (Acts 3: 19).

The Good News was further developed by Peter in his first letter, in which he closely linked man's spiritual salvation with Jesus' death, describing Christians as having been

> *according to the foreknowledge of God the Father . . .*
> *sprinkled with His blood* (1Pet. 1: 2)

> *For Christ died for sins once for all, the righteous for the unrighteous, to bring you to God* (1 Pet. 3: 18)

> *He Himself bore our sins in His body on the tree, so that we might die to sins and live for righteousness; by His wounds you have been healed.* (1 Pet. 2: 24)

The most fully developed teaching about the death of Jesus and His work which makes possible the healing of our spirit is, however, to be found in the writings of Paul.

Firstly, he states that it was God's love for mankind, His grace (undeserved love in action) which motivated Him to send His Son, Jesus, to rescue us from our sinful state:

> *But because of His great love for us, God, who is rich in mercy, made us alive with Christ even when we were dead in transgressions – it is by grace you have been saved.* (Eph. 2:4-5)

and:

> *But God demonstrates His own love for us in this: While we were still sinners, Christ died for us.* (Romans 5:8)

Secondly, he teaches that Jesus had to die upon the cross in our stead, and on our behalf, to satisfy God's just and holy requirement of punishment for our sins:

> *All this is from God, who reconciled us to Himself through Christ . . . God was in Christ, reconciling the world to Himself, not counting men's sins against them . . . God made Him who had no sin to be sin for us, so that in Him we might become the righteousness of God.* (2 Corinthians 5:18-19,21)

> *God presented Him as a sacrifice of atonement, through faith in His blood. He did this to demonstrate His justice, because in His forbearance He had left the sins committed*

beforehand unpunished . . . so as to be just, and the One who justifies the man who has faith in Jesus. (Romans 3: 25-26)

Thus God, in the life, especially the death, and the resurrection of Jesus Christ, has acted in His love to make possible the healing (salvation) of our spirits.

Once again, however, we see that this is not magical, and that our appropriation of the possibility of His healing depends on our response to what God has done for us. We avail ourselves of God's healing work by having faith and trust in what God has done.

For it is by grace you have been saved, through faith – and this not from yourselves, it is the gift of God (Eph. 2: 8)

Therefore, since we have been justified through faith, we have peace with God through our Lord Jesus Christ (Rom. 5: 1)

We know that a man is not justified by observing the law, but by faith in Jesus Christ. So we, too, have put our faith in Christ Jesus so that we may be justified by faith in Christ.

(Galatians 2: 16)

This faith has the essentials which we have already studied:

- **awareness** – now of what Jesus has done upon the cross to reconcile us to God and make possible the healing of our spirit
- **expectancy** – that Jesus will save us
- **assurance** – that all our sins have been entirely cancelled out, that the power of sin has been broken and our spirits healed, and that we are children of God
- **belief** – that we are reconciled to God as we discover this to be true.

It is essentially a **personal**, individual response to the great facts of our salvation. We are personally spiritually sick and need individually to be healed. Even churches which emphasise the act of baptism even of babies, as being means of applying this salvation to the human heart, stress the importance of the presence of faith, firstly on the part of the parents, godparents and church, and eventually in the personal expression, in Confirmation, of faith in Jesus. Evangelicals have serious doubts about this teaching; they feel that it can easily become merely a formal rite and ceremony without a real expression of personal faith, and that baptism should **follow** real faith and be symbolic of a person's salvation rather than the means of effecting it.

It seems, however, from Biblical teaching, that the Christian Gospel was, in the mouth of Jesus and the early apostles, a message to be proclaimed and to which a response of repentance for sin (a real sorrow and turning away from it) and personal trust in Jesus were needed. Baptism, however, in Biblical teaching is very important (Romans 6) as the Christian rite of public testimony and irrevocable commitment to Christ; a real initiation into the truth and efficacy of the Gospel which is best summed up in Jesus' own words:

"For God so loved the world that He gave His one and only Son, that whoever believes in Him shall not perish but have eternal life." (John 3:16).

Chapter 9
The healing of the spirit and knowing God

We have seen that Jesus' life, death and resurrection have made possible the healing of our spirit, and that all this was an act of God to restore the intimate relationship between Himself and mankind. It is through entering into this deep relationship with God that our healing takes place. This Christian healing goes deeper than knowing *about* God's nature as we have seen it revealed to us in His Son Jesus; it comes through a personal relationship which is very real, with the God of the universe, who, Jesus told us, is our heavenly Father. However, before we examine how such a relationship is established, we must study the greatness and the vastness of the God whom we wish to know. Some facts about this God must be given:

- He is **incomprehensible** – that is, His essence and being, as He is in Himself, is and always will be beyond man's understanding. God asserted this truth about Himself through the prophet Isaiah when He said:

    "To whom will you compare Me?
    Or who is My equal?" says the Holy One.

    (Isaiah 40:25)

    and

    To whom, then, will you compare God?
    What image will you compare Him to?

    (Isaiah 40:18)

    and further:

    "For My thoughts are not your thoughts,
    neither are your ways My ways," declares the Lord.
    "As the heavens are higher than the earth,
    so are My ways higher than your ways

and My thoughts than your thoughts."

(Isaiah 55:8-9)

- He is **self-existent**. He did not need to be created and has no origin. This is evident from the Name by which He revealed Himself to Moses when He said: "I AM WHO I AM" (Exodus 3:14).

- He is **self-sufficient** and has no needs of any kind, as Paul points out:

   And He is not served by human hands, as if He needed anything, because He Himself gives all men life and breath and everything else." (Acts 17:25)

- He is **eternal**, everlasting, at the beginning and end at the same time.

   From everlasting to everlasting You are God. (Ps. 90:2)

- He is **infinite** – that is, limitless.

   Great is our Lord and mighty in power;
   His understanding has no limit. (Ps. 147:5)

- He is **immutable** – He never changes.

   In the beginning You laid the foundations of the earth,
   and the heavens are the work of Your hands.
   They will perish, but You remain;
   they will all wear out like a garment.
   Like clothing You will change them
   and they will be discarded.
   But You remain the same. (Ps. 102:25-27)

- He is **omniscient** – He has perfect knowledge of the past, the present and the future and of every individual. So Job describes God as "perfect in knowledge" (Job 36:4) and Jesus taught us that God's knowledge of us is so intimate that

   "even the very hairs of your head are all numbered."

(Matt. 10: 30)

- He is all **wise** – He can devise perfect ends and bring them about by the perfect means. All His dealings with us and all His acts are wise. So Paul describes Him as

> *the only wise God.* (Romans 16: 27)

- He is **omnipotent** – almighty – He can accomplish all that is in His will. John records that the four living creatures in heaven do not stop saying:

> *"Holy, holy, holy is the Lord God, the Almighty,*
> *Who was, and is, and is to come."* (Rev. 4: 8)

- He is **transcendent** – above the created universe, outside it and beyond it.

> *He sits enthroned above the circle of the earth,*
> *and its people are like grasshoppers.*
>
> (Is. 40: 22)
>
> *Surely the nations are like a drop in a bucket;*
> *they are regarded as dust on the scales;*
> *He weighs the islands as though they were fine dust.*
>
> (Is. 40: 15)

- He is **omnipresent** – everywhere; close to; next to; His presence can never be escaped from. Nowhere is this truth more graphically expressed than in Psalm 139:

> *Where can I go from Your Spirit?*
> *Where can I flee from Your presence?*
> *If I go up to the heavens, You are there;*
> *if I make my bed in Sheol, You are there.*
> *If I rise on the wings of the dawn,*
> *if I settle on the far side of the sea,*
> *even there Your hand will guide me,*
> *Your right hand will hold me fast.*
> *If I say, "Surely the darkness will hide me*
> *and the light become night around me,"*
> *even the darkness will not be dark to You;*
> *the night will shine like the day.*
>
> (Psalm 139: 7-12)

- He is **faithful** – all His acts are consistent with His nature and He can be relied on.

  Know therefore that the Lord your God is God: He is the faithful God, keeping His covenant of love to a thousand generations. (Deut. 7: 9)

- He is **good** – kind, benevolent, full of goodwill.

  Good and upright is the Lord. (Psalm 25 :8)

- He is **just** – righteous; meting out justice.

  The Lord within her [Jerusalem] is righteous;
  He does no wrong.
  Morning by morning He dispenses His justice
  and every new day He does not fail.

  (Zeph. 3: 5)

- He is **merciful** – full of pity and compassion.

  "Return, faithless Israel," declares the Lord,
  "I will frown on you no longer,
  for I am merciful," declares the Lord,
  "I will not be angry for ever."

  (Jeremiah 3: 12)

  "Be merciful," [said Jesus] *"just as your Father is merciful."* (Luke 6: 36)

- He is **gracious** – full of love which He shows to the undeserving.

  "For the Lord your God is gracious and compassionate.
  He will not turn His face from you if you return to Him."

  (2 Chron. 30: 9b)

- He is **love** – He wills our good.

  And so we know and rely on the love God has for us.
  God is love. Whoever lives in love lives in God, and God in him. (1 John 4: 16)

- He is **holy** – pure.

  But just as He who called you is holy, so be holy in all you do. (1 Peter 1: 15)

- He is **sovereign** – ruling over all ; free to do whatever

- He is **sovereign** – ruling over all ; free to do whatever He wills; having all authority. This is expressed in the Bible by describing God as King of kings and Lord of lords (Rev. 17: 14).

It is this God, who is so described in the Bible, of whom Jesus says:

"Now this is eternal life: that they may know You, the only true God, and Jesus Christ, whom You have sent." (John 17: 3)

It is obviously very possible for such a God to heal us in every area of our being, and it is in communion with Him that we are healed in our spirits. This knowledge of God, and communion with Him, Jesus taught, is in fact made possible by the Holy Spirit of God who produces in the spirit of everyone who has repented of their sins and put their faith in Jesus' saving work, a new and second birth.

The absolute necessity of this new birth for a living, real, and experienced relationship with God is brought home to us in the conversation Jesus had with Nicodemus in John's Gospel, Chapter 3. As we consider this spiritual counselling interview we must realise that Nicodemus, a "member of the Jewish ruling council", was a very religious, upright and righteous man who not only believed in God and kept the Old Testament Law, but also asserted his conviction that Jesus had "come from God" as a teacher about the truth of God, for as he said, "no one could perform the miraculous signs you are doing if God were not with him" (John 3: 1-2). However, all these credentials were not seen by Jesus as crucial for an experience of a relationship with God within His kingdom. Jesus, in fact, said to him:

"I tell you the truth, unless a man is born again, he cannot see the kingdom of God."

And when Nicodemus expressed his perplexity at this teaching, Jesus re-emphasised and expounded it further by stating:

> "I tell you the truth, unless a man is born of water and the Spirit, he cannot enter the kingdom of God.
>
> "Flesh gives birth to flesh, but the Spirit gives birth to spirit.
>
> "You should not be surprised at My saying, 'You must be born again'. The wind blows wherever it pleases. You hear its sound, but you cannot tell where it comes from or where it is going. So it is with everyone born of the Spirit."

(John 3: 5-8)

Jesus is clearly drawing a parallel between our natural birth from our mother's womb, through the waters (amniotic fluid) of her uterus, into this world, and a second birth into the realities of the spiritual realm through the action of the Holy Spirit within us. So, as before our first birth we were alive, in the womb, but could not experience the realities of this world, though very near to us, until we were actually born; so once we are born of the flesh, we cannot experience the realities of the spiritual realm, even though it be very near to us, until we are born again by the Holy Spirit.

It is apparent from this teaching of Jesus that the healing of our spirit is the work of every Divine Person of the Holy Trinity. We have examined the attributes of the Being of God, whom Jesus taught us to call "Father". Jesus Himself is the revelation of God to mankind and, by His death and resurrection, our Saviour. Now we see that it is the Holy Spirit who actually makes our relationship with God and the subsequent healing of our spirit, real in our experience. As Charles Wesley sang to the Holy Spirit:

> "And make to us the Godhead known
> And witness with the blood."

Through the work of the Holy Spirit within us, giving us a spiritual birth, the Fatherhood of God is not merely a belief that we have, or an abstraction; it is as living and as real a relationship as we could have "in the natural" with any perfect earthly father.

Further to this, the work of Jesus also becomes real to us in our experience. So the work of healing procured for us on the cross becomes for us today an experience of salvation.

Again, we want to join with Charles Wesley in singing:

> Long my imprisoned spirit lay
> Fast bound in sin and nature's night.
> Thine eye diffused a quickening ray –
> I woke, the dungeon flamed with light;
> My chains fell off, my heart was free,
> I rose , went forth and followed Thee!

Similarly on Easter Day, born-again people do not only celebrate a wonderful miracle of resurrection which happened two thousand years ago; they sing of an experience in their spirit:

> He lives! He lives! Christ Jesus lives today;
> He walks with me and talks with me
> Along life's narrow way.
> He lives! He lives, salvation to impart.
> You ask me how I know He lives –
> He lives within my heart.

And when they worship Jesus as Lord, their experience is:

We **see** the Lord;
We see the Lord.
He is high and lifted up
And His train fills the temple.

All this comes back to the fact that the healing process in our spirit begins when we repent of our sins, put our trust in what Jesus has done on the cross, and through the Holy Spirit enter into a living relationship and communion with God.

Chapter 10
The healing of the spirit and the deeper life

We have seen that since the Fall of man we are all born spiritually sick, and this sickness is what theologians call 'original sin'. We have all inherited a sinful nature. This expresses itself in actual sinful thought, attitudes and deeds, and there are also sins of omission: things we should do but do not do.

We have also seen that the healing of this condition was made possible by the life, death and resurrection of our Lord Jesus Christ. He had made possible the forgiveness of our sins and our reconciliation to God. In the last chapter we saw that the healing process begins with our actually entering into a real, living and experienced relationship with God in Christ through a new, spiritual birth, which is the work of the Holy Spirit of God.

However, the Bible and the experience of the Church down the centuries and in the world today, teaches us that there are varying depths into which Christians can enter in their relationship with God in Christ, and that the deeper this relationship is, the deeper also is the healing power of God at work within our spirits. Let us therefore examine this deeper commitment to God as it is shown in the life and teaching of the Apostle Paul.

Paul, or "Saul", as he was called before his conversion to Christianity, was brought up and trained as a devout Jew, an ardent keeper of the Old Testament Law, and of the party known as the "Pharisees" (Acts 23: 6). When he heard about Jews becoming Christians, he at first "persecuted the followers of this Way to their death, arresting both men and women and throwing them into prison" (Acts 22: 4). However, there was a turmoil going on all the time, which is the classic expression of the

70

conflict deep within us caused by original sin. Paul stated this in the words:

I know that nothing good lives in me, that is, in my sinful nature. For I have the desire to do what is good, but I cannot carry it out.

For what I do is not the good I want to do; no, the evil I do not want to do – that I keep on doing. Now if I do what I do not want to do, it is no longer I who do it, but it is sin living in me that does it.

So I find this law at work: When I want to do good, evil is right there with me. For in my inner being I delight in God's law; but I see another law at work in the members of my body, waging war against the law of my mind and making me a prisoner of the law of sin at work within my members. What a wretched man I am! Who will rescue me from this body of death?

(Romans 7: 18-24)

It was whilst in this sinful state that he had the remarkable vision of the risen Jesus Christ, on the road to Damascus (Acts 9) and was called into His service.

For three days he was blind, and did not eat or drink anything. (Acts 9: 9)

Thus Paul, having met Jesus personally, had a good start in becoming a Christian. However, he had to have an even deeper experience of God than this, for the Lord Jesus immediately sent a disciple named Ananias to visit him, and place his hands on him with the words:

*"Brother Saul, the Lord – Jesus, who appeared to you on the road as you were coming here – has sent me so that you may see again and **be filled with the Holy Spirit**."* (Acts 9: 17)

So Saul had to receive, like the apostles at Pentecost (Acts 1:5-8; 2:1-4) and like the Samaritan Christians (Acts Chapter 8) a deeper infilling of the Holy Spirit than they received at their conversion, or new birth. Jesus Himself

71

had promised this to believers, and called it being "baptised [or immersed] in the Holy Spirit " (Acts 1: 5)..

It appears from the account of the belief and practice of the early church as recorded in the Acts of the Apostles, that they always made sure that this deeper infilling of the Holy Spirit had been received. So Paul, later in his ministry, greeted some Christians at Ephesus with the words:

Did you receive the Holy Spirit when you believed?

(Acts 19: 2)

And when they answered in the negative, they were baptised into the name of Jesus, and

When Paul placed his hands on them, the Holy Spirit came on them, and they spoke in tongues and prophesied. (v 6)

It seems from the evidence of Acts, that speaking in tongues was the usual supernatural evidence that the infilling had occurred (Acts 2: 4; 10: 46; 19: 6) and there is no doubt that it brought about a deeper relationship with God in Christ.

If I may interject a personal note into this study of Paul's teaching and ministry, I found this to be true in my own life; for after having become a Christian and being born again in 1952, the act of being baptised in the Holy Spirit intensified my experience of God to a remarkable degree on May 10th, 1969. Believers who have, as **all** should, entered into this blessing have, as I have continually observed,

- a new awareness of the presence of Jesus with them at all times
- a new expectancy of what He will do
- a new sensitivity to hearing His voice
- a new freedom in worship, praise and joy
- a new insight into the meaning and teaching of the Scriptures, which have changed from being, as it

72

were, black and white, to being in colour and three
dimensions
- a new awareness of the reality of the powers of evil
  and, even more, of Jesus' victory over them
- an entry into the experience of and use of the
  supernatural gifts of the Holy Spirit as set out in 1
  Corinthians Chapter 12
- a new release of love for God, the Church, and all
  people, especially the naturally unlovely
- a new release in freedom to witness and talk to
  unbelievers about Jesus.

All of this indicates a deeper life in the Holy Spirit,
who is God, and a greater possibility for the healing of the
spirit to take place.

In considering Paul's teaching and ministry about the
way in which we are healed in our spirit, we must further
examine his words about the absolute depth of dedication
and consecration to God in Christ that he exhibited in his
own life. This can be summarised in his exhortation to the
Christians at Rome:

*Therefore, I urge you, brothers, in view of God's mercy, to
offer your bodies as a living sacrifice, holy and pleasing to God –
which is your spiritual worship. Do not conform any longer to
the pattern of this world, but be transformed by the renewing of
your mind. Then you will be able to test and approve what God's
will is – His good, pleasing and perfect will.* (Romans 12: 1-2)

Paul, of course, was used to the sacrifice of animals on
the altar at the Temple. There, as the life of the animal
was being poured out, the offerer was really saying to
God, "That animal represents my giving of my life, poured
out for you." Now, Paul was saying to the Romans: God
does not look for dead sacrifices, but for **living** ones.

This depth of consecration was expressed by him also in other symbols such as:

I have been crucified with Christ and I no longer live, but Christ lives in me. The life I live in the body, I live by faith in the Son of God, who loved me and gave Himself for me. (Gal. 2: 20)

So **consecration leads to transformation**. In similar vein:

For you died, and your life is now hidden with Christ in God. (Colossians 3: 3)

I well remember reading of a more recent disciple, John Hunt, who went to the then cannibal-infested Fiji Islands as a missionary. On his return his friends asked him, "Weren't you frightened you would die?" He replied, "No, I died before I went!" – A living sacrifice.

This death to self through consecration to Christ, Paul saw as the ultimate means of our spirits being healed from sin. He taught that, through this act of our whole being, we are

> *dead to sin* (Rom. 6: 11)
> *because anyone who has died has been freed from sin.*
> (Rom. 6: 7)

This he linked with the symbolic act of baptism:

We were therefore buried with Him through baptism into death in order that, just as Christ was raised from the dead through the glory of the Father, we too may live a new life . . . . For we know that our old self was crucified with Him so that the body of sin might be rendered powerless, so that we should no longer be slaves to sin. (Rom. 6: 4,6)

No wonder he cried out with joy about the healing of his past:

Thanks be to God – through Jesus Christ our Lord!
(Rom. 7: 25)

and went on to state:

74

Therefore, there is now no condemnation for those who are in Christ Jesus, because through Christ Jesus the law of the Spirit of life set me free from the law of sin and death

(Rom. 8: 1-2)

So, what we can call the 'death' part of Paul's teaching must be complemented by what the infilling of the Spirit can do in the consecrated believer.

About our spiritual sickness Paul says:

The acts of the sinful nature are obvious: sexual immorality, impurity and debauchery; idolatry and witchcraft; hatred, discord, jealousy, fits of rage, selfish ambition, dissensions, factions and envy; drunkenness, orgies, and the like.

(Gal. 5: 19-21)

But, in the consecrated, Spirit-filled believer, a total healing can take place, leading to

love, joy, peace, patience, kindness, goodness, faithfulness, gentleness, and self-control   (Gal. 5: 22-23)

for the death of self has given place to the work of the Spirit, making us more and more in the likeness of Jesus, who is the epitome and supreme example of spiritual health.

Chapter 11
The healing of the spirit and personal devotion

For the healing of our spirit, as taught by Paul, to become a reality in our experience, we must give God time and space in our lives. Most of the Christians we have met during many years of ministry simply allow God to be crowded out of their lives by their everyday cares and activities and then wonder why, after many years as believers, they are still prone to such symptoms of spiritual sickness as impatience and outbursts of anger.

Our being spiritually healed is, in fact, the most important goal of our lives on earth, and yet so many give it so little attention. We have time and space for so many "secular" pursuits and interests; surely we can find time to draw near to God and open our beings to the work of the Holy Spirit, and so allow the process of healing to go on deep within us.

There are three important factors to which we must give our undivided attention on a daily basis for healing to take place: Bible study, meditation, and listening to God. These are the essentials of the two-way inter-relationship which our reconciliation to God, through the sacrifice of Jesus, has made possible. We need to engage in these disciplines because, although Jesus taught that our Heavenly Father knows **us** intimately, we must spend our lifetime getting to know Him better and better and so laying ourselves open to His healing influence.

We know that God, Jehovah, our Father, has revealed Himself to mankind, firstly to the Hebrew people, and then ultimately in the Lord Jesus Christ. This revelation is contained in our Holy Bible, and it is therefore through studying it that we come to a knowledge of God Himself.

Of course, it is important that we read our Bibles and come to know its content, even more so than we would read any other book. We can also listen to it being read to us, for instance in church. However, it is especially important that, in the words of the Church of England prayer for the second Sunday in Advent, we come to the Scriptures saying:

"Blessed Lord, who hast caused all holy Scriptures to be written for our learning: Grant that we may in such wise hear them, read, mark, learn and inwardly digest them . . ."

This exercise involves studying the text of the Bible at great depth, especially in relatively small sections, perhaps with helpful notes, comparing scripture with scripture, and tracing themes through the Bible.

We may do this in groups at a church Bible study which is led by someone able to expound the word, or in homes. However, such group study must not supplant our own getting aside in private with our Bibles and, after prayer that the Holy Spirit will teach us through its pages, studying it for ourselves and for our own edification. In this way we will come to know more and more the nature of God and make ourselves accessible to His healing influence.

When we turn to meditation, however, we are deliberately seeking to enter into the heart and mind of God in an even deeper way than when we, as a first necessity, study the Bible.

In Christian meditation we are seeking to go beyond and behind the written word, or other inspiring subject, to have communion with God Himself. The following is some of the guidance I have given to Christians about meditation:

Meditation on God's word.

It is:
"To exercise the mind in serious reflection, involving the whole of one's being."

Find a place where you can be quiet, relaxed and free from interruption. Some find a church building conducive to meditation; others a bedroom or study.

At home some rise early and use a kitchen or lounge before the rest of the family arrive on the scene. Some meditate walking. **YOU MUST BE ALONE**.

You need your Bible, a notebook and a pen. Helpful aids are a hymn or chorus book, or other devotional book. A prayer book or book of prayers are helpful to some.

RELAX – Take as a key text:
"Be still and know that I am God."

Ask for the help of God the Holy Spirit. Desire Him in love; try to control your thoughts, bringing them back if they wander, by a quiet (not irritable) act of recollection. Try to keep your mind free of care and concern. Speak out the name 'Jesus' once or twice. Read the passage of scripture you have selected – a short one – re-read it several times. Yearn for the presence of God. Memorise any verse that speaks to you. Maybe underline it. Concentrate on **one** subject.

The most important factor in Christian meditation is your sanctified **imagination**.

Imagine you are part of the Bible scene. Lose yourself in His love. Imagine that God/Jesus is speaking directly to you. Be expectant.

FEEL – the peace . . . the healing . . . even the smell and sounds.

APPROPRIATE the promise personally – make it yours. Grasp and absorb what God is teaching you, not only with your mind – but also with your **EMOTIONS** and your **WILL.**

Note the **IMPRESSION** your meditation has made upon you to feed your soul in the future.

Meditations can be long or short. Those you feel have been unfruitful can prove to have been the most worthwhile. Meditation can become a way of life – at any time. You can meditate on all sorts of subjects, e.g. the Name and beauty of Jesus; Psalms; the world of nature; world events from the newspaper.

Rest in Him whom you have already found. If you get carried beyond words just reach out to God – resting in His presence and love. Unite with God by faith.

You experience spiritual healing, grow in grace, pray, intercede and defeat both Satan and sin, more in meditation than anything else you do. God works in you while you rest in Him.

I have taken it for granted so far in this study of the way our spirits are healed through our life of personal devotion, that all Christians pray. By 'praying' it is usually meant that *we* talk to *God*. It is right and healthy that we should do this. We worship Him, praise Him, thank Him for His blessings, bring to Him our personal needs and desires, and intercede for others whom we know to be in need of His grace. However, if we are going to experience healing deep within, then we must give a lot of time to **listening** to Him, for we can be sure that He wishes to speak to us, deep within our spirits, in order to heal us.

Jesus, as we have seen, promised, as the Good Shepherd, that His sheep would hear and recognise His voice (John 10). However, as those who have tried to listen will vouch, it is not always easy to distinguish His voice from the words of our own thoughts, the opinions of others, or the many voices that bombard us from the environment in which we live. Actually to hear God's voice we must have given time and study in order that our "spiritual ears" may be trained.

To elaborate on this need I would draw a parallel between myself as I listen to the birds singing the dawn chorus and the ear of an ornithologist. I simply hear a lot of birds singing in beautiful melody, but the expert has a trained ear, and is able to distinguish the call of a wren, a thrush, a robin, a blackbird, and so on. Likewise when I listen to an orchestra playing a symphony I hear the sound of musical instruments together in harmony; a unified sound. However, the trained ear is able to distinguish, say, a bassoon, a cello, a clarinet, and other individual instruments.

Similarly our spiritual ears can be trained to hear the voice of God speaking directly into our minds and thoughts. His greatest aim in speaking to us is to **heal** us, to reveal the needs of our hearts, and to answer them. As the psalmist said:

> Today, if you hear His voice,
> do not harden your hearts   (Psalm 95:8)

We must especially listen to God through the person of the Holy Spirit **revealing to us where we have sinned** in "thought and word and deed and in things left undone" (Book of Common Prayer) in order that we may confess our sins, and, after feeling the pain, be healed by Him. As John wrote:

> *If we claim to be without sin, we deceive ourselves and the truth is not in us. If we confess our sins, He is faithful and just and will forgive us our sins and purify us from all unrighteousness.* (1 John 1: 8-9)

For most Christians to receive the healing which comes from repentance and confession it will be enough for them to appropriate the forgiveness and cleansing of God on their knees, in private. However, it is also true that a very great deal of release and healing comes from confessing our sins "to each other and pray[ing] for each other so that you may be healed" (James 5: 16). We must remember that Jesus gave His Church power, on earth to forgive sins in His name, and on the basis of the Gospel.

> *If you forgive anyone his sins, they are forgiven; if you do not forgive them, they are not forgiven.* (John 20: 23)

The Church down the centuries has "ordained" certain of its members to hear the confession of sins on behalf of the Church, and, on its behalf, to absolve them. This is all under what it has termed "the seal of the confessional", so that no idle gossip is possible. Many 'Catholic' Christians, including myself, have found the practice of having a preparation time listening to God revealing to them their sins, writing them down, and then confessing them to a minister of the Church, to be extremely spiritually

81

therapeutic. I adhere to the Church of England's teaching about this that "**all** may make a confession, **none** must, but **some** should". Obviously this confession could be to any fellow Christian, counsellor or prayer partner. What is certain is that unconfessed sin is a great barrier to our communion with God and our spiritual healing.

As we are listening to God, sicknesses of the spirit about which we must be honest are: resentment, bitterness and unforgiveness. Our Lord Jesus was very specific, for instance, about our need to forgive from the heart those who have wronged us, no matter how serious such sin against us may have been. His teaching about this even comes into what we call "the Lord's Prayer". There He bids us to say to God:

Forgive us our debts, as we also have forgiven our debtors.

(Matt. 6: 12)

And later He commanded:

"And when you stand praying, if you hold anything against anyone, forgive him, so that your Father in heaven may forgive you your sins." (Mark 11: 25)

Jesus told a graphic parable about a steward who, having been let off a huge amount of debt by his master, flatly refused to release a fellow steward from the comparatively trivial amount he owed him.

"Then the master called the servant in. 'You wicked servant,' he said, 'I cancelled all that debt of yours because you begged me to. Shouldn't you have had mercy on your fellow servant just as I had on you?' In anger his master turned him over to the jailers until he should pay back all he owed.

"This is how My heavenly Father will treat each of you unless you forgive your brother from your heart."

(Matt. 18: 32-35)

Sometimes forgiving others can be difficult, as for instance a wife not only forgiving a husband who has committed adultery but also the woman who seduced him. However, bitterness, resentment and unforgiveness are cancers of the spirit which can, as it were, be fatal.

As we listen to God we must also be guided by Him as to what would be sin for us to do, and what is helpful to our spiritual health. Paul gave us definite guidance about what he had learned from God when he said:

Whatever is true, whatever is noble, whatever is right, whatever is pure, whatever is lovely, whatever is admirable – if anything is excellent or praiseworthy – think about such things.

(Philippians 4: 8)

Certainly we must not lapse into a legalistic relationship with God, for this would bring our spirits into bondage. The burden of Paul's teaching was that a Christian is

not under law, but under grace (Rom. 6: 14).

Living by law, he taught, only strengthens the hold which sin has upon us:

The sting of death is sin, and the power of sin is the law.

(1 Cor. 15: 56)

Yet it is my experience that many Christians, having accepted that they are saved by the grace of God, relapse into a legalistic code of "thou shalt nots" in their walk with God. This is not to say that absolutely every thought or deed is spiritually healthy, but to state that in all our behaviour we should be guided by the Spirit of God, especially in what it means to "love God with all our heart, mind, soul and strength and our neighbour as ourselves", and even more to love others as Christ loved us.

Another lesson to be learned from Jesus is that we must at all times be **real** with God; there must be **no pretence** in our relationship with Him if He is to heal us in our spirits. By pretending we put a thick cover over our real, deep needs; a sort of defensive shell so that the

Lord's grace cannot touch the area of need. Jesus taught this in a parable about a Pharisee and a tax collector. Both went to pray in the Temple, but the Pharisee was hiding behind a shield of self-righteousness, whilst the tax collector laid bare his heart before God, beating his breast and saying, "God, have mercy on me, a sinner."

Jesus said,

"this man, rather than the other, went home justified [made spiritually healthy] *before God."*   (Luke 18: 9-14)

We must at all times be transparent and open to the Lord's healing word or touch.

There are helps today provided by the Church for our spiritual healing, and one of these is the existence of Retreat houses where Christians can spend time in silence, on quiet days or several days of silent retreat. The use of silence is very much part of "Catholic" devotion, but it also has much to teach Christians of all denominations and persuasions. As I pointed out at the outset of this study, we must give God time and space in order that He may heal us. Most Christians must live out their lives in the secular world, earn their living and relate to non-Christians as well as Christians; but we must always get the ultimate goal of our lives in proper perspective: that is primarily that we should be "saved" – made spiritually whole.

Chapter 12
The healing of the spirit and Christian fellowship

So far we have examined the ways in which our spirits are healed from the disease of sin from the purely personal and individualistic perspective. However, as John Wesley once said, "The Bible knows nothing of solitary Christianity", and the teaching of the Bible about spiritual wholeness, or as it can be called, "holiness", is no exception. It needs the fellowship of the Church in order to be perfected and expressed, and the New Testament analogy between life in the Church and membership of a body is of paramount importance for our understanding of growth towards spiritual wholeness. It stands in marked contrast to the emphasis on the personal, individual pursuit of holiness which has characterised Christian devotion in so many evangelical circles. The true, Biblical conception is that Christians grow together, corporately, into the fullness of the stature of Christ.

The teaching that God's primary desire is for a holy people, begins as far back as Moses and his giving of the Ten Commandments (Exodus 20). The theme is continued through all the ritual, ceremonies and the rites of the Temple worship and it was the constant theme of the prophetic voice of God to His people.

In the New Testament, as seen in the epistle of Peter, God transferred this special calling to His new people, the Church. Here, the Church is described explicitly as "a holy nation, God's own people" (1 Pet. 2:9), and Christians are to be holy in all manner of living. It is St Paul, however, who makes the corporate nature of this holiness clear in his letter to the Ephesians. In contrast to a call to a purely personal holiness, he says: "until we all reach unity in the faith and in the knowledge of the Son of God, and become mature, attaining to the whole measure of the fullness of Christ . . .Instead, speaking the truth in love, we will in all things grow up in into Him who is the Head, that is, Christ. From Him the whole body, joined and held together by every supporting ligament, when each part is working properly, makes bodily growth and builds itself up in love" (Eph. 4: 13-16).

When I am teaching on this theme at seminars, I often use a rather mundane but effective illustration. I say that had my mother been a sadist at the time of my birth, she could have cut off my little finger and placed it in a bottle with the necessary preservatives and labelled it "Trevor's Finger". Then, on my coming of age, she could have given me it back as a special present, with the idea in mind that I might have it stitched back on to my hand. Of course, there would have been an obvious problem. It would still have been baby sized! It would not have grown with the rest of my body. In the same way Paul is saying, Christians need an in-depth relationship with each other, in order to share the life of the Holy Spirit, whereby they may grow together in wholeness to the maturity of Christ.

This wholeness, maturity or fullness, about which Paul is teaching is surely that of the love, joy, peace, patience, kindness, goodness, faithfulness, gentleness and self-control, which he declares to be the fruit of the Spirit (Gal. 5: 22-3). These qualities truly describe the beautiful characteristics of Christ's life, and are evidently to be reproduced by the power of the Holy Spirit in the life of His Church through which His life is continually remanifested on earth. It is noteworthy that they are all 'social' virtues, needing in-depth life with others in order to be meaningfully expressed. The life of the Church obviously provides the soil, nurture and environment within which these fruits can come to maturity.

Paul further points out that the primary source of nurture for corporate wholeness is the 'charismatic' or 'Spirit-filled' gifts and ministries which Christ has given to His Church for all ages. (Eph. 4: 11-12; 1 Cor. 12-14). We should therefore be thankful that in recent years there has been a rediscovery by Christians of the importance of these spiritual gifts for the building up of the Body of Christ. Sadly, however, some churches have rejected these insights, and thereby missed out on new opportunities for spiritual growth. Perhaps they have rejected the use of these gifts because modern-day enthusiasts have portrayed them more as personal blessings to be acquired for one's own edification instead of as virtual abilities given by the Holy Spirit for the benefit of the whole community of believers.

There are many charisms mentioned in the New Testament; all are supernatural endowments distributed by the Spirit to whom **He** wills. In his first letter to the Corinthians Paul lists amongst them the word of wisdom, the word of knowledge, faith, gifts of healing, the effecting of miracles, prophecy, the distinguishing of spirits, various kinds of tongues and the interpretation of tongues.

Many books have been written which examine in detail these marvellous spiritual gifts and so I will not do so here. Perhaps, however, one or two Biblical instances of the use of each will portray their nature for the uninitiated.

The **word of wisdom** is displayed in our Lord's reply to those who questioned Him about the rightness of giving tribute to Caesar. Jesus' reply, "Give to Caesar what is Caesar's and to God what is God's" (Matt. 22: 15-22), silenced all His adversaries. In the Old Testament Solomon was richly endowed with this gift from God and it appears that it was abundantly bestowed upon the disciples after the Church received the power of the Holy Spirit (Acts 2: 1-4, 4:13, 6:3).

The **word of knowledge** is portrayed by our Lord's supernatural cognisance of the fact that a woman He had never previously met had had five husbands and was at that time living in immorality (John 4: 17). Peter later was given supernatural knowledge of Ananias and Sapphira's sin of lying against the Holy Spirit, which led to their death (Acts 5: 1-11).

Faith is seen, for instance, in Elijah's unassailable confidence that God would answer by fire on Mount Carmel, and consume the sacrifice he had prepared (1 Kings 18).

Healing is seen in the ministry of Peter as he was certain that God would heal a lame man (Acts 3: 16). Healings themselves are so frequent in the ministry of our Lord and the Spirit-anointed apostles as to need no further mention!

Miracles are supernatural acts other than those related to healing, as for instance when our Lord turned water into wine (John 2: 1-10). They are frequent in the ministries of the Old Testament prophets (*e.g.*, 1 Kings 2: 21).

Prophecy was a frequent occurrence both in the Old Testament and the New, not necessarily in predicting the future, but in declaring the will of God in particular situations. Simeon is one of the first prophets mentioned in the Gospels (Luke 2: 25- 32).

The **distinguishing** or **discernment of spirits** is the ability to test spiritual utterances, or supernatural ministries in order to determine their source. It was such discernment that led Paul to call Elymas a "son of the devil" (Acts 13: 8-12).

88

Various kinds of **tongues** are exhibited in the Old Testament in the various writing on the wall in Daniel Chapter five. It was the first gift the apostles received after their baptism in the Holy Spirit (Acts 2: 1-4) and it is mentioned in this connection in other passages in Acts (*e.g.* Acts 10: 46 and 19: 6).

Interpretation is the ability given to declare the meaning of such utterances, or even the meaning of dreams or visions, as in the case of Joseph (Gen. 41) and Daniel (Dan. 5).

Other spiritual gifts and ministries mentioned by St Paul may seem less sensational, but are just as important for the proper nurturing of the Church. They are 'helpers', 'administrators' (1 Cor. 12: 28); service, teaching, exhortation, leading and showing mercy (Rom. 12: 6-8); evangelists, apostles and pastors (Eph. 4).

In every case of a spiritual gift or a ministry (the constant ability to exercise some particular gift) except that of tongues, Paul emphatically states that the gift is given to be used for the common good and building up the Christian community as a whole (Eph. 4: 12). Tongues alone, he says, can be used for the edifying of oneself, when used in private. Paul enjoins however, that when the gift of tongues is used "in Church" it **must** be followed by interpretation, so that once again the principle of mutual edification may be fulfilled (1 Cor. 14).

Spiritual gifts then, are given to believers according to the sovereign will and disposition of the Holy Spirit. It is not wrong, however, to seek them (1 Cor. 12: .31, 14: 1). as long as the purpose is for the **well-being and spiritual wholeness of the whole Church.** In the realm of spiritual gifts, states Paul, the Body of Christ, like the human body, maintains a condition of interdependence (l Cor. 12).

Many of these gifts obviously have been used through-out the whole history of the Church for the nurturing of the Christian community. Clearly no Church could ever have functioned without adequate pastoral care, teaching, and the ministry of the word and sacraments, together with such everyday ministries as administration, helps and service. However, all too often, those who exercise these ministries are tempted to rely more upon their natural endowments rather than the power of the Holy Spirit.

On the other hand, the gifts which could not function at all without supernatural empowering, such as tongues (with interpretation), miracles, prophecy and healing, have been sadly neglected throughout Church history. Men of such calibre as St Augustine, Martin Luther and John Wesley have all stated that this has never been because God has impoverished His Church by withdraw-ing the gifts, but rather that the Church has not had enough faith to use them!

The use of the spiritual gifts, however, is not the only input believers need in order to become whole spiritually within the Christian community. As we have seen, the fruits of the Spirit are all social graces and depend upon relationships with others in order to mature. For in stance, I know that I am a man who abides in real peace and has a lot of patience, as long as I am alone, and no one tests these areas of my life too severely! Within the community of believers, however, these graces have often been tested and thereby, I trust, have matured. For all of us however, this only appertains if the community is a close enough group for the necessary purging to take place (John 15: 2).

Before I was baptised by the Spirit I was vicar of more than one church where problems between those who frequented the building were few. This was not because those under my care were especially mature individuals; rather, I believe it was because they and I had not responded deeply enough to the Spirit for us to be close enough together to have any problems! In a truly British manner, my people shook hands, and arm's length was as near as they ever came to each other either spiritually or emotionally!

However, when, for instance, the Spirit began to move at the Church of St Paul, Hainault, as the people responded to Him, they were drawn ever closer together. This togetherness was expressed in our house meetings, aptly called "Growth Groups". It was in these closely-knit fellowships that patience, love, goodness and the other fruits of the Spirit really began to be evident. When personality problems arose, the inevitable tendency was to want to run away from the difficulties of what 1 called "growing pains"! We soon discovered, however, that the way to spiritual maturity was not to withdraw from deep fellowship with others, but to go through personality clashes into wholeness.

I remember especially an occasion when the Church's voluntary verger was given an opportunity of growth through very unfortunate circumstances. Our church building: was so small, and our Tuesday evening congregation so large, that she was called upon to set out scores of chairs in empty spaces every morning before the "big meeting". She did so faithfully and well. However, one week, due to administrative mistakes, she was asked by three of us, in the course of the day, to keep rearranging them. I was the person actually to make the third request, without knowing that she had moved all the chairs twice before! She exploded with righteous indignation, and resigned. Later, I explained to her that, within the community of believers, God had given her the choice of either using what had happened as material for life-long resentment and bitterness or as material for patience, kindness and love. She responded to the Spirit; took back her service for the Lord, and matured spiritually as a result.

So we see from all the teaching of the New Testament that the first essential for growth in spiritual maturity is the existence of the Church, the Spirit-filled Christian community, living together in Him. It is only within such a community, with each member responding to the gifts and graces of the Holy Spirit, that real spiritual growth can come about. Conversely, it is only as the individual Christians each mature, that the whole body grows into the fullness of the measure of the stature of Christ. Charles Wesley put it very well when he wrote:

> He bids us build each other up,
> 'Til gathered into one;
> To our high calling's glorious hope,
> We hand in hand go on.

> And if our fellowship below
> In Jesus, be so sweet,
> What heights of rapture shall we know,
> When round His Throne we meet!

Chapter 13
The healing of the spirit and Christian perfection

In our study of the healing of the spirit through our relationship with God some theological words have emerged. One of these was the expression 'original sin', denoting the nature of the spirit's sickness, and another was 'justification', or 'being declared righteous or innocent, through our faith in what Jesus did for us on the cross'.

Now we come to another such theological word: 'sanctification' which is the process by which our spirits are healed, or, to use yet another word, are made 'holy'. This is the in-depth work of the Holy Spirit as we open ourselves up to Him and to one another. The question we must now face is whether or not this work can become 'entire sanctification' or complete healing and holiness, this side of eternity.

The witness of the Church down the centuries is to the fact that holiness or wholeness of the spirit **is** attainable in this life. The 'Catholic' Church has, however, indicated that this is a rare state to reach spiritually, because although it has "canonised", or "declared to be saints" a lot of outstanding Christians, they are in fact few, compared to the number of Christians who have lived since the first century AD.

There has, however, been a belief among Protestants also that this state is attainable. So John Wesley, commonly thought of as primarily an evangelist in the eighteenth century, declared that, "the people called Methodists have been raised up to spread **holiness** through the land." All Methodists were urged to believe that entire sanctification or "perfect love" as Wesley also termed it, was possible through faith in God, and John Wesley wrote a book especially propagating this belief.

The desire for this blessing amongst Methodists was put into song by John Wesley's brother Charles in such words as:

> The thing my God doth hate
> That I no more may do.
> Thy creature, Lord. again create
> And all my soul renew.
>
> My soul shall then, like Thine,
> Abhor the thing unclean
> And sanctified by love divine
> For ever cease from sin.

And:

> The most impossible of all
> Is, that I e'er from sin should cease;
> Yet shall it be, I know it shall.
> Jesus look to Thy faithfulness;
> If nothing is too hard for Thee,
> All things are possible to me.

Also:

> O for a heart to praise my God,
> A heart from sin set free,
> A heart that always feels Thy blood
> So freely spilt for me.
>
> A heart in every thought renewed
> And full of love divine,
> Perfect and right and pure and good,
> A copy, Lord, of Thine.
>
> Thy nature, gracious Lord, impart,
> Come quickly from above;
> Write Thy new name upon my heart:
> Thy new, best name of love.

This belief was expressed succinctly in a prayer to the Holy Spirit:

> O come and dwell in me
> Spirit of power within!
> And bring the glorious liberty
> From sorrow, fear and sin.
>
> The seed of sin's disease,
> Spirit of health, remove,
> Spirit of finished holiness,
> Spirit of perfect love.
>
> Hasten the joyful day
> Which shall my sins consume . . .

The Wesleys felt that these views were absolutely Biblical, and certainly our Lord commanded us to be

> *"perfect, as your heavenly Father is perfect."* (Matt. 5:48)

and would He have commanded the impossible? Paul refers to:

> *as many as are perfect* (Phil. 3: 15 *NASV*).

He says that he wants to

> *present everyone perfect in Christ* (Col. 1: 28)

and he agrees with the prayer:

> *that you may stand perfect and fully assured in the will of God* (Col. 4: 12 *NASV*)

and Peter writes:

> *But just as He who called you is holy, so be holy in all you do;* (1 Peter 1: 15).

Personally, I know that I have not yet experienced such healing of my spirit as to be entirely sanctified, and I have not, in all my ministry, met anyone of whom I would unhesitatingly assert this to be true; and yet surely it is within God's power and will to accomplish this complete healing of our spirit. It is certain that too many Christians settle for being justified and do not trust God in opening themselves to His Spirit and reaching out for entire sanctification. We should never settle for less than God's best: our complete spiritual wholeness.

Although I have never met anyone who would claim to be completely spiritually whole (and should anyone in any case ever claim to be perfect?) I have seen wonderful marks of God's healing power in the spirits of men and women to whom I have ministered and whose testimony I have later heard as to what God has done in their lives.

I well remember "Barbara" standing in front of me awaiting ministry at St Paul's Church, Hainault. She looked a wreck of a woman: bent, shaking and smelling of alcohol. She was, she explained, a prostitute who used men in order to get drink, and men used her to satisfy their lusts. Her child, which she treasured, had been taken from her by the Social Services as they felt she was unfit to be able to look after her.

That evening "Barbara" accepted by faith what Jesus had done to make possible her forgiveness and reconciliation to God. She was very spiritually sick and in great need. However, it was, for her, a new beginning. In the ensuing weeks our Church cared for her, and she opened her life to the healing work of the Holy Spirit. She was healed from her alcoholism and became an assistant matron at an Old People's Home. The last time I saw her, a few years ago, she had had her child restored to her loving care and was happily married to a Christian man.

Then there was "Barry", an escaped prisoner, on the run from Armley jail in Leeds. He decided to find "sanctuary" in our church. He had burgled many homes;

but, like "Barbara", he was reconciled to God that night, through trusting in the saving work of Christ. His first act was to "give himself up" and return to the prison to serve the rest of his sentence. He, too, opened up his life to the work of the Holy Spirit. He started a Bible study for fellow prisoners in the jail, and ten men regularly attended. Such was the extent of healing in his spirit that he was released early and worked for the Lord in the Leeds City Mission. One of the prisoners whom he led to Christ was also so spiritually transformed that he is now a Pentecostal Pastor.

A week before beginning to write this chapter I was preaching and ministering at a church in Dover. After the service a middle-aged lady ran to me on the platform.

"I want to tell you," she said, "that when I first came to you for help some years ago I was a hopeless heroin addict and also an alcoholic."

She went on to explain to me that at that time she had dropped to 8½ stone in weight and was near to death.

"I accepted Jesus as my Saviour and you ministered the Holy Spirit into my life. I was immediately released from all my addictions without any withdrawal symptoms, and I have been a Christian ever since. I am now a leader locally in the Women's Aglow movement."

She looked radiant; full of the Holy Spirit.

So I have seen the healing power of the Holy Spirit working miracles of transformation not only in these three people, but, down the years, equally so in the lives of many hundreds of sin-sick souls who have come to me seeking salvation and the baptism of the Holy Spirit. I have kept in touch with many over the years and seen them grow and develop into whole, mature, and even holy men, women and young people.

The Bible's teaching about the power and will of God to heal the spirits of sin-sick souls has, in my experience, been abundantly manifested not only through my own ministry and that of my wife Anne, but also in the scores of wonderful testimonies I have heard in the United Kingdom and many other parts of the world. In the realm of the Spirit:

He is able to do immeasurably more than all we ask or imagine, according to His power that is at work within us.

(Eph. 3: 20).

PART FOUR

The healing of the soul

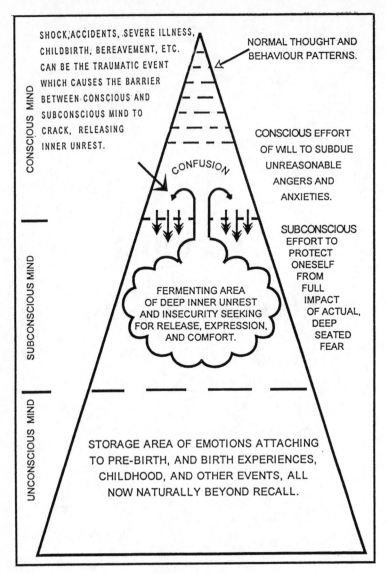

DIAGRAM B

Chapter 14
Sickness of the soul

The soul, as we saw in diagram A, (page 24) comprises our mind (our thinking capacity) our emotions (our feelings) and our will (the force that drives us). It is, like the spirit, to use a philosophical word, 'metaphysical'; that is, it is not a solid piece of matter. Thus when anything goes wrong, for example, with the brain, it can be scanned to find the source of the trouble. However, this method of diagnosis cannot be used on the soul, because it is not a physical entity.

The method used by secular psychiatrists to diagnose what is wrong with the soul is called psychoanalysis, which literally means 'an analysis of the soul'. The methods of psychoanalysts vary according to which school of thought (*e.g.* Jungian or Freudian) the practitioner has given allegiance; but I would maintain that the spiritual approach I am advocating in this section of the book is really the only one which brings total healing to the soul.

What I do accept from the insights of psychology in the 19th century is that the soul consists of various depths, as shown in diagram B (opposite). Some Christian teachers don't like to admit that they accept these "worldly" insights, and instead talk about the "healing of memories", the "healing of the hidden self", or "soul healing". But, whether they realise it or not, they are, as we shall see, harmonising with, and not negating, the insights of the classical psychoanalysts Freud and Jung.

What is certain, whether from a Christian or secular standpoint, is that we all have a 'conscious' soul or 'mind'. This is the level which consists of everything of which we are conscious moment by moment. For instance, I am conscious of the fact that I am in my study, sitting at my desk, paper in front of me, electric lights on and my mind focused on the thought of this chapter. What is actively engaging the conscious part of our soul; what is uppermost in our mind, emotions and will can vary hundreds of times each day.

Below the level of the conscious mind is the area of the 'subconscious'. This is full of memories which are more or less easily recalled. However, we push down into deeper levels of our subconscious minds incidents or experiences in our lives which have caused us insecurity, hurt, emotional pain, stress or even fear, which we want to forget. Of course, there are pleasant, happy and joyful memories at this level as well, but these do not cause the soul to be lacking in peace – which is the essence of soul-sickness; it is the painful and frightening experiences which in fact cause us to be sick in our souls. This is because, even though we may have succeeded in forgetting these incidents or conditions in our lives, the emotions which they evoked still live on at this depth of our being.

So the subconscious mind, at its deepest, can be full of insecurity, anxiety and even fear. We try, and usually manage, to keep this cesspool of soul-sickness out of our conscious thought and feeling, but at times of conscious insecurity or stress; or through some traumatic event such as one or more of those described in the diagram, these feelings and emotions come to the surface as feelings of fear, depression or anxiety, and we latch these feelings on to all manner of thoughts, causing us in turn to feel depressed, over-anxious or desperately fearful. We may experience attacks of sheer panic, develop phobias such as agoraphobia so as to be afraid of even going out of our home; claustrophobia – terrified of being enclosed or "shut in"; hypochondriasis – desperately concerned about our health; the possibilities are almost limitless.

Not only can we feel insecure and afraid because of what is bubbling into consciousness from the subconscious mind; there may also erupt into our emotional life, experiences which happened to us in our infancy, time of birth, or pre-birth experiences which are by nature totally beyond our ability to recall. These emotions bubble up through the subconscious part of our soul, into our consciousness and we become depressed, anxious or fearful without being able to comprehend at all why we are in such a state. Each of these, psychologists term a 'neurosis'. We are sick in our souls and know ourselves to be so, and often desperately cry out for help.

An even worse state of soul-sickness is what psychologists term 'psychosis'. This is a condition when we are very sick but do not know it. In this state the soul has been in so much pain that it has used defence mechanisms in order to escape the torment. Thus it seeks to live in an unreal world (schizophrenia) or goes from extremes of depression into a very excitable or "high" state (manic-depression) when irrational and excessive excitement can lead to bizarre behaviour.

Further problems can arise from our sickness of the soul which are not particularly of the mind or will, but become problems of the spirit or body. In the realm of the spirit the sufferer can be convinced he or she has committed an unforgivable sin, is being punished or even rejected by God and is cut off from fellowship with Him. The sufferer often feels to have an intense *spiritual* problem, when actually the problem is in the soul and not the spirit. However, the sufferer is caught in a spiritual-soul-emotional syndrome wherein depression leads to feeling rejected by God, which causes deeper depression and fear, resulting in feeling even more rejected by God, and so the problem gets increasingly worse. This is because the relationship between soul and spirit is, as we saw in diagram A, very close.

Not only, however, is the soul intertwined with the spirit; it is also closely related to the body. So soul-sickness produces an effect on our physical condition. Fear in our souls causes the heart to beat faster, paleness of appearance, sweating of the skin, churning in the stomach and other physical symptoms which cause us to be even more anxious, and we may become fearful of fear itself, and so are caught up in another syndrome: this time of the body and soul, which can affect our whole physical and soul health, and may bring a sufferer to the point of contemplating suicide as the only way of escape from what has become like torture.

It goes without saying, in passing, that one who is so sick in soul and so lacking in peace will suffer from insomnia, as the soul can find no rest. Chemicals are also released into our nervous system which affect its whole functioning, including the chemicals such as metanonin, which balance the brain, and so our whole being is affected by soul-sickness. We do well to cry out, "Who will deliver me?!", and thankfully there is an answer in the healing nature of God.

Chapter 15
Healing ministry to the sick soul

During the twenty years since we have been ministering healing to people with all kinds of needs, Anne and I have seen hundreds of soul-sick sufferers wonderfully healed by our Heavenly Father in the Name of our Lord Jesus Christ. One of the ministries which has brought deep peace to many has been the ministry of confession and absolution.

We have already looked at this ministry in relation to the healing of the spirit. However, because the spirit and soul are so closely related, I have found that when folk are carrying a burden of guilt in their spirit, it very seriously affects their mental peace, and frequently has caused sufferers to be depressed in themselves and volatile in their relationships with others.

Of course, it is possible, and it is in fact the experience of most Christians, that they can accept their forgiveness and cleansing from guilt by confessing their sins privately to the Lord and receiving by faith all that He did for them upon the cross (see page 59). However, in the cases of not a few, this guilt either remains in the conscious part of the soul, or is simply pushed down into the subconscious area where it causes such deep stress that the pathological symptoms I have described in the last chapter, erupt into the consciousness. For these people the way of confessing their sins to a Christian brother or sister, and being prayed over for forgiveness, is the only way to bring relief.

I am thankful personally that I have learned a great deal from all Christian traditions, and my experience is that auricular confession of sin and guilt to a priest or minister is the very best solution to our guilt problems. Thus our unburdening of ourselves is under the seal of the

Confessional and the absolution from guilt is pronounced by a man (or woman) who is ordained by the Church to do so on its behalf and is experienced in giving further counsel and advice to the penitent. I not only make my confession whenever I feel the need to do so, but I have also heard many confessions in the years of my ministry. Sometimes this hearing of confession occurs in the "healing line" at an open Christian meeting, even in Pentecostal churches, or, as I prefer, following the traditional pattern in an Anglican church or in the privacy of a home. As an ordained Anglican I know I have the authority of the Church, on the basis of the work of Christ, and on its behalf to pronounce absolution.

Many such sufferers spring to my mind, whose confessions I have heard, including both sexes, all ages and all classes of people. They have confessed every imaginable sin, from sexual sins like lesbianism and adultery to impure thoughts, sins against mother, father or children; anger; lust; pride; vanity; misuse of money; theft, and so on. Many have felt condemned and even unclean, burdened with guilt, and all have been struggling with real problems in the area of the soul. I have led each of them through a simple form of confession in private and strict confidentiality.

"Bless me," they have asked, "for I have sinned." Then each has continued: "I confess to God Almighty, Father, Son and Holy Spirit, that I have sinned exceedingly in thought, word and deed, through my fault, my own most grievous fault. Especially I accuse myself of the following sins:".

They have then gone on to state what their sins actually and specifically were. They have concluded with the words:

"For all these sins and those I cannot now remember, I am heartily sorry and intend to do better. I ask of you, my Christian brother, counsel and absolution in Jesus' name."

I have then said:

"On the basis of the work of Jesus Christ on the cross, your penitence, and the authority given me by the Church, I absolve you from all your sins. Go in peace, for the Lord has put far from you all your sins; and pray for me, for I also am a sinner."

The release brought by these words cannot be exaggerated. I have kept in contact with many of these people whose confession I have heard, and know that they were deeply healed in their spirits and souls.

A much more usual ministry in which Anne and I have engaged for the healing of sickness of the soul has been that of the "laying on of hands", always accompanied by the spoken word which has addressed the seeker's need. We have already seen that this was the normal way Jesus and His apostles used to bring healing from heaven to those who came to them (page 28). We have had prodigious testimony to the efficacy of this ministry, usually exercised in public meetings.

The first person I ever ministered to in this way for the healing of the soul was Carol. At that time she was aged twenty-four and was undergoing a terrible "nervous breakdown". She described her healing to a newspaper reporter as follows:

"My marriage broke up nearly three years ago and I took it very bad. I spent some time in a psychiatric hospital. I returned home dependent on anti-depressant tablets and sleeping pills.

"I used to hide in my room and chain smoke all day. My mother told Mr Dearing about the state I was in and he persuaded me to come along.

"I can't remember doing it, but I went forward. Mr
Dearing laid hands on me and prayed for me.

"When I walked out of the church I found the
nearest drain and threw my tablets down it.   I
realised God loved me and had healed me."

Carol said, "Prayer saved my sanity." She went on to
qualify as a nurse and was awarded the matron's "Nurse of
the Year" prize. She is now married to a Pentecostal
pastor and has had no return of her illness.

The following are further testimonies to the effectiveness of this ministry:

Mrs M B wrote to us:

"So I was invited that evening to attend the Service at
Hesketh Bank Methodist chapel, where I hoped to
discuss my problems with you, and that evening I did
go forward, as I also had been a sufferer from
depression for five years. I was set free! Now six
weeks later I feel alive and have emerged from that
dark tunnel of hell where I was for three years
without even a glimmer of light."

Miss CMS wrote from Nottingham:

"I thought I'd write and tell you about a touch of
healing I had at the service where you were
ministering at on Wednesday evening at Bulwell
Pentecostal Church. Mrs Dearing prayed for me as
I've had nervous trouble for many years.   I
mentioned that I'd had a lot of stress due to the work
I do with the charity I helped to start; Mrs Dearing
prayed for me and during the prayer asked the Lord
to heal me of the depression I'd had. I realised that
the Lord must have guided you to ask this, Mrs
Dearing, as I hadn't mentioned the depression I often
used to get, especially when waking up in the

morning. Since the prayer I've not had any depression at all."

From A M at Sevenoaks, Kent:

"The Lord brought me to your meeting at City Hall.
There Trevor was moved to ask my son and myself to
come forward from our seats at the back of the
gallery, as the Lord had a special ministry for us. You
laid hands on us with prayer and I want you to know
that I have been wonderfully released from deep
fears which had been passed through several
generations. I really feel new now and believe He
has set me free."

From Isobel:

"I felt released from emotional hurts the afternoon you
ministered to me Anne, I sleep much better now and
am coming off sleeping pills."

From Charles:

"For three years I have steadily deteriorated with
depression to such an extent I was even envious of
those in prison who were much better off than me,
trapped in my own prison. Now praise the Lord I am
healed and have been leaping about like the lame
man healed by Peter."

On one occasion when ministering to a depressed lady
I felt led to accompany the laying on of hands with an
anointing with oil. This was in the case of Marcia, a pretty
clergyman's wife with four children. She had become
deeply depressed after the birth of her fourth child. She
was due to see her psychiatrist the day after the meeting
and knew that, humanly speaking, a fourth admittance
into a psychiatric hospital was inevitable. Her illness was

so acute that she had to take massive doses of medication, but life was still intolerable.

Marcia was too distressed to move out of her pew to receive ministry, so I laid hands on her as she sat in the choir stalls, sobbing. After the ministry she became peaceful, and I asked her to come forward to receive further ministry with anointing of oil.

She said afterwards that as she felt the oil running down her face it helped her to drink in more and more of the power of the Holy Spirit. She emerged a transformed woman.

The psychiatrist was amazed at the remarkable change in his patient, who was now filled with joy and happiness. She was immediately able to manage without her tablets, now also able to look after her family and support her husband's ministry with confidence. In a television interview some time later she said it had taken Jesus just half a minute to heal her.

These are just a few samples of testimonies we have received and miracles of healing of the soul we have witnessed through direct ministry to afflicted people. The healing has always been immediate and enduring the tests of time and the normal stresses of life.

Chapter 16
Soul healing and the exposure of painful experiences

Not everyone suffering from sickness of the soul is healed so immediately and dramatically by Christian ministry as those mentioned in the previous chapter, and I am not persuaded that it is God's perfect will always so suddenly to heal. This, I believe, is because He desires to perform a deeper work in us. In any case, although we all, because of the Fall of man, suffer in some degree from sickness of the soul, not all, thankfully, become so pathologically ill as those with the symptoms I have described.

Nevertheless we can **all** benefit and reach a deeper level of peace, joy and happiness by the measures we take to co-operate with the healing work of God. I shall outline this in the present chapter and the rest of this section on the healing of the soul. This is because we all have strong painful emotions locked up in the subconscious and unconscious minds, ready to break through into consciousness if we suffer undue stress or a traumatic experience in our lives.

I frequently teach at healing sessions that nothing which is hidden can be healed. Every painful thought and experience, or, as we have seen, even sin, which we have gone through in our lives, must be brought from the darkness, as it were, of our natural beings into the light of God's presence if we are to be made totally whole. In the case of the healing of the soul this means that everything which is causing deep unrest in the depths of our souls must be brought into consciousness.

Psychoanalysts (not psychiatrists) are trained in methods of how to bring into the consciousness the experiences which are causing us stress, strain or mental

pain from the depths of our souls. A **Christian**
psychoanalyst (preferably professional) can be a real help.
especially if we are really sick, and I have heard of no
problems with Christians using their services. A good,
Spirit-filled, mature and prayerful counsellor can also be
of considerable help. However, I am convinced that we
can engage in this healing exercise on our own, in a
private and quiet place as we seek the help of God.

In order to do this we must get alone with God,
thinking about Him in the Person of our Lord Jesus
Christ. We must realise that His knowledge of us and
interest in us is so real and personal that, as Jesus said,
even the number of hairs on your head are known to Him.
He is our Heavenly Father who loves us, and His perfect
will is to make us totally whole. It is, however, God in the
Person of the Holy Spirit, who will reach into the depths
of our souls.

We need to have paper and pen ready to write down
what He reveals to us from the depths of our being. Our
prayer must be:

> Search me, O God, and know my heart;
> test me and know my anxious thoughts.

(Psalm 139: 23)

Then we must be quiet before Him, as He brings into our
consciousness a painful experience which has affected the
health of our souls. As He does this, we must first of all
write down, as best we can, just what this experience in
fact was.

Next, we must lie back and **actually re-live it**, facing
perhaps the experience of rejection, insecurity, or pain.
At this moment the temptation is to try to forget the
experience, not face up to it, or push it down; but we
must, as far as possible, go through it again. When
counselling at these times I have known sufferers cry out,

shed many tears, or even, in extreme cases, scream in agony; but we must let our emotions really burst into expression and let ourselves go.

Secular psychoanalysts are expert in bringing a person to this point, but then, sadly, they have no way of dealing with the pain. It is true that bringing the experience, or memory, into the conscious mind is in itself therapeutic, but the secular analyst cannot in any way bring the healing to the soul of which God is infinitely capable.

So, in his or her pain, the Christian seeker will bring the experience in prayer to God, and lay open his heart to the ministry of the Holy Spirit. Some Christians have found it helpful for healing to see Jesus, as they picture Him to be, coming into the experience, and just seeing what He will do to relieve the hurt and pain.

Personally, I have found the Biblical account of Jesus ministering to Peter by washing his feet (John 13) very helpful, for I myself, when counselling, tell the sufferer to **feel** and **hear** Jesus ministering to them in love, with His hands and His words. He spoke peace to a raging storm (Mark 4) and "there was a great calm". So He will also speak **peace** to the storm which we are now bringing to Him and which lies deep within our hearts. We must **take our time**, giving Jesus time and space completely to heal the pain.

Another Biblical incident I have found helpful is for the sufferer to picture the man who was journeying from Jerusalem to Jericho, who was beaten and robbed by thieves, who left him lying on the road helpless and half dead. Then we see Jesus, the Good Samaritan, **coming to where he was**, exactly as described in the parable, **pouring in** the balm of soothing, healing oil (a symbol of the Holy Spirit) and the antiseptic wine, the healing agent for festering, deep wounds.

113

It is important that we stay with our healing Lord, in the Person of the Holy Spirit, for as long as it takes us to feel a deep peace; the sort of peace Jesus meant when He said:

> "Peace I leave with you;
> My peace I give you.
> I do not give to you as the world gives.
> Do not let your hearts be troubled
> and do not be afraid." (John 14: 27)

I believe it is important that we let the healing balm of the Holy Spirit sink, as it were, deep into us for a few days, before going through this healing exercise all over again until we really feel the deep pain in our souls, going back even to birth and pre-birth experiences, which the Lord will, in time, reveal to us to have been fully healed.

If we are actually counselling someone whom we are leading through deep hurts, we can in fact suggest these Biblical pictures to them and give them Jesus' promise of peace. It is important also that the counsellor "lays hands" on the sufferer and speaks and prays the peace of God into his heart.

God's perfect will is the total healing of our souls to their deepest depth.

Chapter 17
Soul healing and Christian meditation

In the same way as asking God to expose and heal hidden pain in the depths of the soul is a therapeutic spiritual exercise, so too, Christian meditation on scriptures which promise healing is also a practice in which we should all participate. It will bring in-depth peace to our hearts in these days when the speed of life is so fast, pressure intense and stress a common experience. Even more important than this is the fact that this type of prayer will bring in-depth healing by God into the hidden recesses of the soul.

When we engage in this pursuit of peace there are two important promises about the Word of God with which we must begin. The first is that:

> The word of God is **living** and **active**. Sharper than any double-edged sword, it penetrates even to dividing soul and spirit, joints and marrow; (Heb. 4: 12).

The double-edged sword was the sharpest weapon known in Biblical days. We can today liken it to the sharpness of a surgeon's scalpel. What this scripture is stating, therefore, is that the Word of God can reach the very depths of our being; the division between soul and spirit. It can therefore penetrate into the very depths of our soul, reaching down to pre-birth experiences.

The second is the promise:

> So is My word that goes out from My mouth:
> It will not return to Me empty,
> but will accomplish what I desire
> and achieve the purpose for which I sent it.
>
> (Isaiah 55: 11)

Here indeed is a precious promise! We are going to meditate on God's Word and it **will** accomplish His healing will in our souls. We can draw a parallel here between medication a doctor may prescribe and what happens in our souls when we absorb the Word of God. The tablet we take is prescribed to accomplish a certain result in, say, our body. It also has chemical substances which have power within them to accomplish this end. So the Word of God has a purpose: to bring us healing deep within our souls, and it is also a **living** and **active** Word, containing within it the power to accomplish this very desirable result.

To absorb God's word we must set aside at least fifteen minutes every day, in a private room where we will not be disturbed, having shut ourselves in, to be alone with God. We remember Jesus' words that God sees in secret and will surely be with us (Matt. 6: 6).

We must sit or lie down, relax our bodies but concentrate our minds on God, remembering that He is very near. We take a text of Scripture, learn it by heart and repeat it aloud several times. Then we go over it repeatedly, emphasising and thinking about the meaning of each different word or phrase, applying the text to ourselves.

We may take, for example, Philippians 4 v 13: "I can do everything through Him who gives me strength."

We first of all learn this scriptural promise by heart, and then reflect on it again and again, confessing that *I* – me in all my need and weakness, trepidation and fear – can do everything through Him – Christ – who gives me strength. Next we emphasise the word **can** – there is no doubt about it – I *can* do everything through Him who gives me strength. Then emphasise the word **everything** – nothing, not even the daunting task I face today, is excluded. Eventually we begin to absorb the fact that this is **through Christ** – spend time thinking about who He is and what the Gospels show He can do – and that nothing is impossible for Him to accomplish. Then we reflect on the fact that, for this issue or task which is so unnerving or frightening, He **will give me strength** – I am not going to undertake it in my own weakness, but in **His** strength.

We must meditate on this text for several days in order to absorb its truth and its unfailing promise. We will recall all it means when we feel inadequate, weak or fearful or face a task which we feel unable to accomplish. This will mean for an agoraphobic, for instance, going to the shops as on a holiday.

There are many other promises God has made which we can learn and on which we can meditate. To take another one. God has promised:

"You will keep 'me' in perfect peace, because 'my mind' is steadfast(ly directed towards You), because I trust in You"   (Isaiah 26: 3).   (Notice I have legitimately personalised this text to make it applicable to myself.)

Again, we learn it by heart and repeat it aloud several times. Then – word by word:

You – we meditate on who God is in His infinite power and love

will – the absolute certainty of the promise

keep – the unfailing permanency of the promise

me – despite my fearful, troubled state of mind

in perfect peace – what is **perfect** peace? – It is without lack or hindrance – then relax and **feel** the peace flowing into you and over you

my *mind is steadfast*(ly directed to You) – fixed upon God with no distractions

because I *trust in You* – as I trust in God I can be assured of His perfect peace.

Or, slightly differently, Jesus said:

> *"Come to Me, all you who are weary and burdened, and I will give you rest. Take My yoke upon you and learn from Me, for I am gentle and humble in heart, and you will find rest for your souls."*   (Matt. 11: 28)

Here Jesus is picturing a yoke of oxen dragging a very heavy load up a hill. Do I feel burdened like that? Am I labouring under a load of care or depression I feel I cannot bear? I grasp the invitation to come to **Jesus**, and think of all that He is and has meant to millions down the centuries – He is **gentle** and humble in heart – and now this invitation, "Come" is addressed to me. What does it mean to "**take His yoke**"? – it means to be under His direction and care. He promises me rest – for my soul. I feel this rest – deep down rest – in the depths of my being – utter relaxation and restoration – rest from anxiety, care and fear. I feel Him lifting my load from me – I can run up this hill now – I am at peace, I am happy and life is much easier with **His** yoke upon me.

Other texts (personalised) I suggest for use in this kind of meditation are:

"I will wait in hope on the Lord and He will renew my strength. I will soar on wings like an eagle; I shall run and not grow weary, I will walk and not be faint."
(Isaiah 40: 31)

"I will cast all my anxiety on Him, because He cares for me." (1 Peter 5: 7)

"The eternal God is my refuge, and underneath are the everlasting arms." (Deut. 33: 27)

118

"He is able to do immeasurably more than all we ask or imagine, according to His power that is at work within me." (Ephesians 3: 20)

"His peace He leaves with me, His peace He gives me. My heart will not be troubled, neither will I be afraid." (John 14: 27)

"I will not fear, for He is with me; I will not be dismayed, for He is my God. He will strengthen me and help me; He will uphold me with His righteous right hand." (Isaiah 41: 10)

"When I call upon God He will answer me; He will be with me in trouble, and He will deliver me and honour me." (Psalm 91: 15)

"God has redeemed me and has called me by my name. When I pass through the rivers, they will not sweep over me." (Isaiah 43: 1-2)

"God did not give me a spirit of timidity, but a spirit of power, and love and self-discipline." (1 Tim. 1: 7)

And there are many more you can find or be shown.

I have suggested to many people over the years that they meditate in this way and have taught them how to do it. Testimonies have come back to me by the score that even pathological cases of soul-sickness have been healed through such meditation on God's Word, and all of us will find deep rest and peace in the midst of hectic, sometimes stressful lives if we meditate like this at the beginning of every day. It is an important aspect of the search for total healing.

Chapter 18
The healing of the soul and Christian counselling

We have seen in a previous chapter that a Christian counsellor can be of real help to the healing of the soul, especially when a seeker is asking God to reveal the pain which lies in the depths of his or her being. Anne and I have counselled scores of people during the course of our ministry. Many have testified as to how in-depth counselling has brought them into a new realm of wholeness. One such person is "Joyce". She wrote to us of her experience as follows:

"First of all I must give some background. Since my second child was born in 1957, I have had severe bouts of clinical depression, some lasting many years. I have been in hospital on some occasions and had treatment and many different types of drugs – anti-depressants etc. Latterly I have developed arthritis in both hips and the spine.

"When the following spiritual experience happened to me I was in a terrible state – very suicidal – because I could not stand the depression and could get no relief.

"I had been going to church and Communion and crying out to God – 'help me' – nothing seemed to happen.

"On July 15th at our morning service at St George's, Stephen had been preaching about the Holy Spirit. He invited people who wanted to receive the Holy Spirit, or a further release to stand up and he said that he would pray with them. I stood up and said the prayer after Stephen. Then the Lord spoke to me – He said: 'You do not <u>have</u> to be mentally ill –
    You do not <u>have</u> to have arthritis.'

"I believe He was saying to me that you *can* be overwhelmed with these things if you allow yourself to be – but there is no need – there is another way – I **will** help you and care.

"On the following Tuesday I had an appointment to see the Reverend Trevor Dearing, an Anglican clergyman who had had periods of mental illness during his life – has been cured – and has a healing ministry both here and in America.

"The Lord released me and I was able to talk to Trevor – previously I had not been able to tell anyone how I felt, not even my husband, or Stephen or my Christian psychiatrist – all because of the fear that if I said I was suicidal I would be put in hospital. After listening to me Trevor said that he would like to anoint me with oil – he did this and prayed for me.

"About two days later I became ill with constant vomiting. We called the doctor who said I must take nothing but sip ice cold water. I did this for ten days and lost one and a half stone in weight. I did not take any drugs because I could not keep them down. I had been on at least six painkillers a day for arthritis. I had also been taking anti-depressants and lithium. Since then I have not taken any of these things, just an occasional painkiller, maybe one in three or four days. MY DEPRESSION HAS COMPLETELY GONE – I AM AT PEACE, healed, restored, forgiven, a completely different person. Thank you Lord.

"Bishop Maddocks said 'Healing is Jesus meeting us at our point of need' which is just what the Lord did for me – Greatly is He to be praised."

This healing was the result of a combination of listening, counselling and ministry.

I believe, in these days of increasing pathological soul (commonly called mental) sickness, the Lord is calling more and more mature Christians to be counsellors. In my opinion counsellors must, however, have the following qualifications in order to be used in this healing:

- They must, themselves, not only be "religious" and "churchgoers", but must have a personal relationship with the Lord Jesus.
- They must have been baptised in the Holy Spirit and be conversant with and use some of the supernatural gifts of the Holy Spirit described in Chapter 12.
- They must spend time with the Lord in personal devotions each day and listen to, and be able to hear, His voice.
- They must know their Bibles very well, especially teaching texts and Biblical incidents related to Divine healing of the soul.
- They must be full of supernatural love, especially for the unloved and severely afflicted.
- They must have faith in God's will and power to heal.
- They must have learned lessons themselves from the experiences of life.
- They must be good, patient listeners.
- They must themselves be active church members and relate to others, and be accountable not only to God, but to an elder, minister, bishop, or other Christian leader for their ministry.
- They must be Christians who have themselves sought and received at least a good measure of wholeness from the Lord.

As I have stated, Anne and I have had vast experience in successfully counselling those who have sought the healing

of their souls from the Lord, through us as his instruments. We have learned a great deal through experience
and would pass on the following suggestions to
counsellors, remembering that this ministry will require
love, time and patience as the Holy Spirit reveals the
causes of soul-sickness and moves, through us, to heal
deep emotional needs.

- When anyone requests counselling, Christian
  counsellors must make it **very** clear that they are
  dedicated Christians and will counsel as such; that it
  is no use coming for secular opinions, as the
  counsellor will be offering a spiritual solution to the
  need.

- Counsellors should not take on too many seekers
  after healing at one time. The ministry is very
  demanding and it is better, unless one is a full-time
  professional counsellor, to take on only one or two
  people at a time, with whom one can deal in a
  relaxed and unexhausted manner. Counsellors
  must be firm in rejecting too much work. Even
  ministers, priests and pastors do well to train others
  in their congregations to counsel, and delegate the
  work to them as full-time Christian ministry, for
  this, as I know well, makes many other types of
  demand on one's time and energy.

- Counselling sessions should have a definite time-
  limit which is strictly adhered to – say one or one
  and a half hours at the longest. Counselling sessions
  can, as I know to my detriment, go on and on, from
  need to need, and in the end become almost aimless
  and very confusing, because usually needy people,
  especially those suffering from neurosis, will talk
  and talk and talk until the counsellor is weary and
  the real object of the exercise may even be lost. So

it is better to have several one-hour sessions than one whole day.

- Counsellors must be convinced that it is God's will, no matter how long it takes, to bring deep peace and soul-health to the person being counselled. If this is not so, then it is useless even to begin.

- Every counselling session **must** begin with prayer in the presence of the "patient". Such prayer is best uttered extempore and should ask God for the gifts of wisdom, knowledge and discernment for the counsellor, and for His presence during the time spent together; petition should be made that the "enquirer" may be brave enough to be absolutely frank and honest and be open to God's healing power, and that the results of the session will be the further extension of God's Kingdom and healing for all the sufferer's needs; all to the glory of God.

- At a first session it is often best to begin with relatively "small talk" about, say, the weather, how long the person's journey took, their family, work etc. This sets the patient at ease and helps him to see that the counsellor is also at ease and is a "natural" person.

- Eventually counsellors have to **listen** as the sufferer is encouraged to talk about themselves, their fears, phobias, feelings, problems, panics etc and to describe, sometimes in answer to a question or two, or a bit of prodding, what **they** believe to be the source of their trouble. The history of their Christian life should also be explored from its beginning to the present time. Counsellors, as they listen, will have their ears open to the voice of the patient but will also be listening deep down to God.

125

- Here real discernment is called for, because frequently the problem being described is not the *real* problem. The sufferer may, for instance, present what they see to be spiritual problems when really they are suffering from clinical depression. The counsellor must discern whether such things as fears are rational or irrational. If, for instance, they are irrational, then they are probably a symptom of much deeper insecurity, conflict, guilt, fear of failure or of rejection. The counsellor must also discern whether there are any relationships or circumstances which are promoting soul-sickness.

- Counsellors can then begin the process of delving into the memories, hurts, conflicts or guilt which lie deep down within the soul, asking God quietly in their hearts to reveal the **real** needs.

- It is important that counsellors try to turn the eyes of the patient from their own needs and weaknesses to focus on Jesus and His revelation of the love and power of God, and to teach the person helpful scripture passages and texts and to teach them how to meditate. (Jeremiah 31: 3;   Deut. 33: 12-16; Psalms 34 and 121; Isaiah 41: 10; Ephesians 3: 14-21 and Phil. 4: 13 are worthy of study.)

- Then is the time to seek even more co-operation from the sufferer, who, the counsellor has become sure, really **wants** to be well and is not simply using their need constantly to seek attention.   Jesus Himself once asked a very sick man: "Do you want to get well?" (John 5: 6). This cannot be taken for granted and, if necessary, the patient must be faced with the possibility that, maybe without realising it, they have a part of them which *needs* their sickness. The patient must be encouraged to relinquish negative thought-habits and rituals and take positive steps forward based on God's sure promises (see Num. 23: 19; Josh. 21: 45; 2 Cor. 1: 20; 2 Tim. 3: 16). At this stage counsellors must be patient and not, for instance, criticise an inability to trust God, because deep inner healing is often needed before faith can be released. It is important session by session that the sufferer keeps a notebook of "victories" and together with the counsellor, praises God for progress.

● Counsellors should not give too much advice in one session; a distressed mind has a limited capacity to hear and act. Counselling may be required for a long period of time, and the sufferer must never be allowed to feel abandoned. Even when counsellors reach a conclusion that God's work and purpose have been fulfilled, patients must always feel that they can come back for help should the need arise.

● **Every** counselling session must finish, as it began, with prayer. The laying on of hands and sometimes anointing with oil are a means of applying all that has been learned and also of channelling the grace and healing power of God into the sufferer's heart and life. Counsellors should speak the peace of God into the storm which may be raging deep down in the patient's soul. Prayer (or absolution) can be offered for cleansing from guilt and also for the healing of wounds and memories. Counsellors can ask God to give strength to resist and fight fears, to proclaim liberty from bondage and the opening of the door of the prison of depression, all in the Name of Jesus.

In closing I would mention two particular problems which have constantly arisen in our own counselling sessions. The first is the ability of someone who feels very guilty to accept the forgiveness of God, but then find that they cannot forgive *themselves*. At such a time it must be pointed out that the problem is, in fact, an inverted form of *pride*. The person is really saying to themselves, "I am really, basically, too good a person to have acted in that way." This problem must be addressed by the counsellor pointing out how desperately sin-sick the human heart really is; that we are all, by nature, capable of the most heinous of sins and that we cannot be saved by our goodness, but only by casting ourselves on the endless, matchless grace of God.

A second problem is that people, even Christians, particularly if they are suffering from depression, frequently have a very low self-esteem, do not even like themselves, and often wish that they were someone else. Such a problem must be tackled by referring to the fact that Jesus Himself taught us to have a right kind of self-love and that this is not sin. He said, "Love your neighbour **as** yourself", not "Love your neighbour and *not* yourself". Sufferers must be taught from Scripture (*e.g.* Ephesians Chapter 1) that they are not in the world by accident, but that the birth was planned by God and that their individuality is precious in His sight. I have often said to a patient:

"God made you and He doesn't make junk."
Teaching on God's love for each individual being so great that He gave His only Son for each and every individual, including the person now in question, is also very helpful.

Finally, counsellors should watch out for self-pity in emotionally afflicted people. It is the most soul-destroying and disintegrating of attitudes towards one's condition or circumstances that I have met. That a person may have had a very bad time or endured more than most must be admitted, but it should also be pointed out that there are many people in the world who would gladly change places with the self-pitying individual. Thankfulness to God for every blessing must be taught, and through dedicated Christian counselling the sick soul can experience and will experience the total healing of God in Christ.

PART FIVE

The Healing of the Body

Chapter 19
Divine healing and our bodies

When we are whole in spirit and in soul we shall be much healthier in our bodies. This is because, as we saw in diagram A (page 24) our spirits, souls and bodies are so inter-related. Is the health of our bodies, however, so very important to God?

We have seen in our Biblical studies that Jesus, God incarnate, spent a great deal of His time and energy during His ministry, bringing bodily health to those who came to Him in sickness, physical infirmity and affliction. This in itself portrays the interest God has in our physical well-being.

In Bible days there was a belief, made widespread through Greek and pagan religions, that the human body was, in itself, inherently evil and that the aim of salvation, in any form, was to release our good spirits and souls from the evil influence of the body in which they were encased. This widespread view was called 'gnosticism'. It was a very commonly held belief, and influenced the thought of many early Christians. The teaching that God, the Supreme Good Spirit, could take on a human body, was abhorrent to these people and therefore they began to teach that, in Jesus, God had only *seemed* to take on flesh. This viewpoint was termed 'docetism'. The apostles, in their writings, were very urgent in their contradiction of this heresy. So John wrote:

> *That which we have heard, which we have seen with our eyes, which we have looked at and our hands have touched – this we proclaim concerning the Word of life.* (1 John 1: 1)

and:

> *Many deceivers, who do not acknowledge Jesus Christ as coming in the flesh, have gone out into the world. Any such person is the deceiver and the antichrist.* (2 John 1: 7)

John further says:

> *This is how you can recognise the Spirit of God. Every spirit that acknowledges that Jesus Christ has come in the flesh is from God* (1 John 4: 2)

So, by God Himself taking on flesh, He has shown that the human body is not evil but very important to Him, for although it is fallen, it was designed and created by Him.

Paul's teaching also contradicts the gnostics and docetists, and shows how holy and important our bodies are when he writes to the church at Corinth:

> *Do you not know that your body is a temple of the Holy Spirit, who is in you, whom you have received from God? You are not your own; you were bought at a price. Therefore honour God with your body.* (1 Cor. 6: 19-20)

Paul teaches in this particular chapter the fact that at the return of Christ in glory we shall be given new, **spiritual** bodies which will no longer suffer any sickness or decay, but this is in the future. For now, we must seek the maximum health of our physical bodies, as best we can, until the day that we die, or, if it is sooner, Christ returns in splendour and ultimate victory.

We seek this health, which, as we have seen, is important to God, by obtaining medical help when we are sick or in pain (I have added an appendix to this book about the place of physicians and medicines in the Christian life) and this is right and proper.

However, as we have seen in previous chapters, God has provided 'sacramental' ways by which His health and life-giving Spirit can permeate the body and bring health to it until it is His will, perfectly to heal us in spirit, mind and body, by taking us from this life into heavenly realms. This ministry, as we have seen, is a very important part of the full Gospel ministry of the Christian Church to the whole person. To these means of grace and some results of them which Anne and I have witnessed in our ministry we will now turn.

Chapter 20
Divine healing of the body and the laying on of hands

Anne and I must have ministered the laying on of hands to thousands of sufferers since we felt called to the healing ministry in 1970 (in my case) and discovered that we were particularly gifted in this realm by the Holy Spirit. We prefer to minister to people in an atmosphere of praise and worship, in the company of as many believers as possible and after I have preached the Gospel of the Kingdom of God. This is in the context of a "Gospel-Healing" Service, although we have ministered in the middle of, or at the end of, the traditional and even formal services of whatever church or fellowship we happen to be in.

Public ministry like this we regard as the norm for us. However, we have ministered to people privately in their home or ours, after making sure the "patient" is actually a Christian or after having explained to them the Gospel message of Jesus as Saviour. In any case we have had testimony to many sensational or not so remarkable healings of every different kind of need imaginable.

We see the laying on of hands today as entirely Biblical and a commission of the Lord Jesus Christ to us within our membership of the Church. We do it in obedience to His command. We see the laying on of hands as a God-ordained point of contact between the sufferer and the power of the Holy Spirit, who has promised to heal in the Name of and for the glory of Jesus Christ. We do not feel, and in fact, have not experienced, a sense of power flowing through our bodies or hands. As we minister we emphasise that it is what is taking place between the sufferer and the risen Christ, on whom they should be concentrating their faith and attention, which is of the most vital importance.

We sometimes pray a prayer of faith over the seeker, believing for and claiming a miracle which we believe Jesus has promised. We do not usually use "if it be Thy will" prayers because we are sure in ourselves that our God is the One who moves to heal the needy. If we were not sure of God's will then we would not minister in the first place! We believe that "if it be Thy will" prayers are destructive of faith. We only pray on those lines if a person is dying and we sense that it may well be the time God has chosen for him or her to depart this life – and this need not be at the age of seventy or over.

Usually, however, we do not pray at all because, as was pointed out in previous studies, we believe that this ministry should be an authoritative one, and therefore we command sicknesses to go and bodies (or parts of them) to be healed in the Name of and according to the promises of Jesus. We have received hundreds of testimonies to the efficacy and power of this ministry. Some of them are as follows, including some letters sent by post, testifying to the healing of blindness:

Mrs I.M. writes:

> "I came out to you for healing prayer. I was blind in my left eye and almost in my right. It was the next day I was healed of blindness and later I realised my migraine was also gone after 44 years. The next morning I was able to look at the sky without my dark glasses. I never wore them again. The Lord had healed the retinas of my eyes."

G.M.J. wrote from Southend-on-Sea after the laying on of hands:

> "I was almost blind in my left eye and all the doctors said there was nothing they could do. I thought no

136

more about my eye. On the Monday morning I awoke and thought there was something funny about my eye. I could see, I could see! I was dancing and singing and phoning everyone."

E.L. wrote:

"With God all things are possible and through the power of Jesus Christ, the ministry of Trevor Dearing, and the prayers of several hundred people, sight has been restored to my blind eye. No medical explanation is either feasible or possible and it only remains for me to give joyful thanksgiving to our Lord Jesus Christ."

And S.L.:

"I was at the Saturday night meeting at Gatley, and really enjoyed Trevor's message. I went up for healing. That night my left eye clicked and when Paul examined my eyes we both noticed that whereas the left one had been slightly sunken, they were now both level with each other. The right one looks very clear and the left one is now showing a pupil. The other night we were out in the car and I was able to see the street lights and I was thrilled!"

Limbs, and especially backs have been healed. A vicar wrote from Scotland:

"Our oldest member received relief from pains in her legs so much so that she can now lift her foot about two inches higher than before. Last week she was able to get out of my car unaided. A young man from the Baptist Church received healing for his hand, injured in a saw mill accident about eighteen months ago."

G.F.:

"It was your wife who actually prayed for me. Not only was I completely healed of severe degenerative arthritis of the spine but also of an intense abdominal pain."

J.C.:

"The Conference was a wonderful blessing. My back and spine has felt fine since Trevor laid hands on me for healing. My posture feels straight and I am no longer trying not to lose my balance."

Another vicar wrote:

"One lady came to the church for the first time on Sunday night to your meeting. She was healed and gloriously saved. She surprised the lady in the post office when she went to collect her Social Security money. She had not been able to walk for weeks and weeks."

A lady in Wisbech, Cambridgeshire, had been housebound for over two years and was literally carried to the meeting. After receiving the laying on of hands she wrote:

"My sticks I have loaned to a young man recovering from a broken leg. I can sleep through the night and can jump out of bed. I have skipped with a rope, run the length of my path with my dog, played trains with my grandson and even ridden a bicycle. I want to tell the whole world what Jesus has done for me."

G.B. writes from Lowestoft:

"I do thank you for the prayer that you said for the healing of my arm and wrist, and praise the Lord that I was healed. When I went to physiotherapy on the Monday following, the therapist was so surprised that I could do so much more. I was able to tell her that it was the Lord I had to thank for the healing. I was discharged from the clinic and am now driving my car again and am able to carry on with the wirk that the Lord has given me to do for Him."

R.Z. from Birmingham:

"Since the prayer for my neck and shoulder I have had painless nights, after treatment from physiotherapy and drugs were of no avail. I have had great relief since that night at Hockley."

B.D. from Derby:

"Oh the joy it gave my husband John and myself that the Lord touched both the people we brought to the meeting. Molly was back delivering babies . . . she took her corset back to the hospital and told them to give it to someone else. Jesus has also healed my back!"

Mrs R.O. from York:

"The baby Darren you prayed for at Pollington about 14 years ago who couldn't kick at one year old is now a beautiful teenager, strong and healthy. Since that day the Lord touched his body and joined his back to his legs – a real creative miracle!"

Dennis Houghton of Skegness wrote his testimony:

"When I was 23 years of age I was a lorry rounds-man which was heavy work carrying 17 stone sacks of corn. On one particular day I was carrying a sack of corn into a barn when the bag hit the top of the door and I lost control of it . . . I felt something snap in my back which left me in a semi-paralysed state. After six months of continual pain things had gone from bad to worse. The hospital specialist told me spondylitis had set in and that by the time I was forty I would be bent over.

"At that time Trevor Dearing was holding monthly meetings at Stamford. When the night came I felt too tired to go but my wife Joan was persistent, so I went. It was a cold night when Trevor prayed for me but I felt a deep heat penetrate my body. I sank to the floor under the power of the Holy Spirit. We went home and Joan helped me to bed as I was feeling completely shattered. It seemed like the end. I had tried everything and nothing had happened. Next morning however, much to my great surprise I was able to dress myself and didn't need any more pain-killing tablets. The Lord had wonderfully healed me. I found I could now run up the office steps, play football, cricket and tennis with my teenage boys."

We have also experienced many healings from epilepsy. A pastor, for instance, recently wrote:

"The sister of Mavis our OHP projectionist has not had any more epileptic fits since you prayed for her. She was having them very frequently prior to this. Another lady in our fellowship who is waiting to have an operation on her stomach has had no more pain since having ministry."

The healing of organic illness has also been common-place through the laying on of hands. J.R.L. wrote to a friend recently:

"I believe Trevor was used in the healing of my lovely son Duncan. I went to a healing service he was running when Duncan was desperately ill as a baby and he's never looked back."

V.B. wrote:

"I just want to let you know that Jesus healed me in both areas that Trevor prayed for. When I went to get my blood pressure checked this morning I was allowed to discontinue the wretched pills! And then I went to the eye man and he was left speechless at the improvement. In both cases I was able to witness and say that I knew I had been healed when

I was prayed for. Now I feel like shouting it from the roof-tops!"

A vicar's wife wrote from Cornwall:

"Helen was quite ill with some kidney disorder and came to the evening service. You prayed with her, Anne. She has been well since; two weeks later she came forward in our evening service for salvation. Little Zoe, the baby Trevor prayed with on the Sunday morning, was wonderfully healed. Another 18 month old baby had meningitis and tonsillitis and was rushed into hospital a month ago, but praise the Lord was in and out of hospital in 3 days. His mother was born again last Sunday week."

We have been especially gifted in ministering to couples who could have no children. There has been much testimony that, after ministry, babies have arrived. A typical example are Anna and Roger:

"I was told we would never have a child. I had already lost two, then I'd lost one tube and the other tube was blocked and kinked and badly damaged. I tried many operations and was told to forget it. You ministered to me. I was due to go into hospital to try a test tube baby. When the day came they were on strike and I was mad. What I didn't know then was that I was already having a baby. She's lovely. Her name is Penny. It's a real miracle. The doctors had a shock."

Recently at a meeting a man stood up to say that he and his wife were told they would never have children. They had every form of treatment known to the medical profession including trying to fertilise the egg outside the womb. All this was without success. They spent over £2,000 on private treatment – in vain. However, he stated that Anne and I laid hands on them and prayed, and now they have three children to the glory of God!

Cancers too have yielded to this ministry. A lady phoned us recently to say that she had cancer of both breasts when she came to us for ministry many years ago. She was completely healed by God and is now eighty-three years of age. She has had no return of the malignancy.

Our ministry of the laying on of hands, which is usually accompanied by an authoritative word of command, was also used by the Lord in another case of cancer, that of Nanette Pierce. This lady was wheeled into a meeting suffering from terminal cancer. She was a dark, pretty young woman, married with two children. Her tragic condition was well known in her home town of Peterborough because the local newspaper had issued a special appeal to readers to bring her home from the USA so that she could die and be buried there.

The cancer was in her spine and she was confined to the wheelchair. However, some months later the newspaper carried a front page headline:

MIRACLE

Reporters described how this young lady was no longer expected to die. After I had ministered to her at one of my meetings in Stamford, doctors discovered that all traces of her cancer had disappeared.

She told newspaper reporters that the change had actually taken place when I had gone over to her and commanded: "Rise and walk in the Name of Jesus!"

"I couldn't help but obey him," she had confessed, "I just got up."

So a lady who looked such a pathetic wreck, rendered paralysed by cancer, stood and then walked for the glory of God. She had heard the word of God, unhesitatingly responded and had been healed.

So then, our ministry has proved beyond doubt that God is interested in our physical, bodily health and that where there is obedience to His Word, a powerful ministry and the response of faith, He will bring total healing to our bodies.

Chapter 21
Divine healing of the body and the word of knowledge

There are occasions when God uses the power of His word to bring healing without there being any laying on of hands at all. This is through the "word of knowledge" which Paul lists in the supernatural gifts, in his first letter to the Church at Corinth (Chapter 12). There are special times, usually at public meetings, when I flow in the Spirit of God and these words simply pour from my mouth. To function in this way I have to be under a special anointing of the Holy Spirit which usually comes upon me immediately after I have preached or as I am ministering the laying on of hands to the afflicted. I suddenly have images or revelations about a certain condition impinging on my thoughts.

They seem to come into my mind from nowhere and, in faith, I share about the condition from which I am sure someone in the meeting is suffering. The revelation is very specific and not simply, for instance, that someone present has a bad back. The Lord would, in such a case, indicate to me the exact area of the back, the nature of the pain, how long the person has been in pain and how, if through an accident, the condition actually came about.

As I share one word of knowledge like this, then others will follow in quick succession. I ask the sufferers who are being addressed by the Holy Spirit to stand, claim their healing, and praise the Lord for it. Then, just as suddenly as the revelations started, they will stop coming to me and I know that they are at an end. I can never simply "turn them on", and I would know in my soul and spirit if I was simply engaged in guessing. One newspaper reporter who was present when I was flowing in the Spirit in this way termed the ministry "healing by remote control".

Here are some testimonies which I have received to the effectiveness of this supernatural ministry to the glory of God. Dennis Rose, who lives in the Stamford area, sent me the account of his healing as follows:

"In November 1973 at the age of 44 years I became seriously ill with kidney problems and was taken to Stamford hospital, where I remained for 12 days. In the weeks that followed I was in great pain and feeling very weak. I began to despair of ever feeling well again. Having always been strong and healthy this was a new dimension in my life.

"One Friday I was reading the Stamford and Rutland Mercury, and in it was the following:
Divine Healing Service in the Congregational Hall, Stamford, led by the Reverend Trevor Dearing.

"I was not very keen on going, but I felt so ill I was prepared to try anything. My doctor was doing his best to help me, but to no avail. I told my wife Iris about the advertisement I had seen in the paper and she was not at all interested. She wanted me to be perfectly well again but did not want to be involved in that sort of ministry. All through her life she had been staunch Church of England, and liked the comfort and dignity that went with the Service.

"On the 7 mile journey I kept wondering if I was doing the right thing, for I was also Church of England though not as staunch as my wife. I arrived at the meeting at 7.00 pm for the 7.30 start. The Congregational Hall was filled very quickly. I sat at the back, ready to make my escape. I still hadn't convinced myself I had done the right thing. I really was very nervous.

"What followed was wonderful. Trevor Dearing began the service with prayers that made me realise that here was something special. They were spiritually uplifting. The tone was set, the chorus and hymn singing divine, and for almost two hours Trevor preached about the love of Jesus for mankind. It was a joy to listen to him, and as the words flowed he made the New Testament come alive.

"This was followed by the laying on of hands. People just fell down under the power of the ministry given by Anne and Trevor Dearing. This was the Lord's work through the power of the Holy Spirit. I witnessed many wonderful things and it was too much for me to understand. I did not go forward for ministry, still being too nervous. This was all new to me and I returned home amazed at what I had seen.

"I repeatedly spoke about what I had witnessed and was longing for the next service in a month's time. I went to the following three services and was still afraid to go forward for the laying on of hands, although I was still in a lot of pain and feeling ill, not knowing how I would feel after the ministry.

"My wife finally agreed very reluctantly to come with me in case it was necessary for her to drive me home. This was the fourth meeting and I was going forward for the laying on of hands. Iris and I arrived at the Congregational Hall and it was full. Many people were ill and in great need, and I was one of them. The meeting started. After prayers, choruses and hymns Trevor started to speak about the needs of the sick and suffering people. He suddenly stopped and said, 'There is someone in the congregation who is in great pain on the left side below the rib cage and has been ill for a considerable time.' He also said that the person had been afraid to come forward, but that the Lord was healing him right where he was, and there was no need to come forward.

"I knew immediately that that person was me. I felt a warmth go through my body from my head to my feet and all my pain went with it. Within a very short space of time my feelings of illness went also. I must also mention that prior to Trevor's word I had noticed that Iris was raising her hands in praise to the Lord. She said that she had never seen or heard anything so spiritually uplifting as the singing and outpouring of praise as she witnessed in the Congregational Hall on this her first visit. We praised the Lord at that evening service and continue to praise Him to this day.

"I informed Trevor of my healing and that his word of knowledge had been for me. Iris and I continued to attend the monthly services, becoming more and more involved with the passage of time. I was privileged to be used in stewardship and ministry at many meetings. We continue to serve the Lord and to witness His Divine healing and blessing on many people's lives. The meetings were a period in our lives which brought us great joy and a deeper awareness of the presence of the Lord. The glory is the Lord's. To the Father, Son and Holy Spirit be all honour, glory and power, praise and dominion for ever!"

There are, during this ministry, occasions when healed people just cannot restrain themselves from immediately praising the Lord.

"My foot! My foot! I can move it! I really can!" shouted an excited girl in a marquee at Cheadle where I was ministering.

She had cause for joy, as her club foot had not moved since she was born and she was actually awaiting an operation with only a slight chance of success.

"I can hear!" deaf people have exclaimed – and so the miracles have multiplied.

One woman wrote:

"I would like to pass on some news of a miracle of healing that came to me at Wisbech, when, by word of knowledge, you described my symptoms. After keeping away from doctors for three years, I suddenly needed six within the space of three months, and was taken ill when away from home and had to send for help. Constant bilious attacks, a colitis condition and agonising pain in the small of my back – sometimes causing me to lie on the floor to try to find a position to be out of pain. The night before Wisbech I spent hours with a 'waterworks' condition exactly as you described it. From the moment you mentioned these symptoms they vanished completely. I still did not believe it and had arranged for a check-up at the RAF hospital. After a week of intensive investigation they pronounced me completely free and healthy."

Another:

"We praise the Lord for the wonderful disappearance of a lump in a lady's breast which was feared to be malignant. By word of knowledge you said it would go – and it has!"

Also, Mrs S.N. of Basildon had healing of memories through a word of knowledge on Canvey Island. She had been distressed for years by the memory of the loss of her son. Now she has peace. Praise the Lord.

A letter from Stoke-on-Trent described how I had revealed the healing of four major illnesses.

"You also discovered a bad chain forged between a mother and child which you promised would be broken and you said 'there will be nothing but love from now on.' That chain had been growing heavier and thicker between my daughter and me. She came home for Christmas and the love has been wonderful."

From Spalding came a letter:

"You said, 'There is a person here who has been suffering from sinus trouble for fifteen years.' That was me. You declared me healed, so I threw away my drops. The sickness just went. Praise the Lord!"

Letters followed from my visit to St John's Church, Bradford, telling – among other things – of the "healing of someone on my right having trouble with his rectum" and another with a "relationship with a difficult mother".

And so it has gone on for over twenty years. I never prepare or know beforehand what the Lord is going to reveal to me but I am obedient to speak out in faith all that I believe He is showing me, and great has been the glory to His Name in hundreds of miraculous healings.

Chapter 22
The healing of those who are absent

We have seen in our Biblical studies that the usual way God moves to heal the sick is through direct ministry to them by one or more of His servants. This is the Biblical norm, whether the ministry is in a church building, a home, or even in the streets. However, there are three instances in the ministry of Jesus when sufferers were healed by Him across miles of distance when petitioners came to Him on their behalf.

One occasion is when He healed a royal official's son. The official came to Jesus, and "begged Him to come and heal his son, who was close to death." He said to Jesus:

"Sir, come down before my child dies."

Jesus replied, "You may go. Your son will live."

The man took Jesus at His word and departed. While he was still on the way, his servants met him with the news that his boy was living.

When he inquired as to the time when his son got better, they said to him, "The fever left him yesterday at the seventh hour."

Then the father realised that this was the exact time at which Jesus had said to him, "Your son will live." So he and all his household believed.

(John 4: 46-53)

A second time this "absent" healing took place was when a centurion came to Jesus asking for healing for his servant who was paralysed and "in terrible suffering".

The centurion had faith enough to believe that Jesus did not actually have to go to his house to perform the miracle. He said to Jesus:

"just say the word, and my servant will be healed."

When Jesus heard this, He was astonished and said to those following Him, "I tell you the truth, I have not found anyone in Israel with such great faith."

. . Jesus said to the centurion, "Go! It will be done just as you believed it would." And his servant was healed at that very hour.

(Matt. 8: 5-13)

The third instance of Jesus healing at a distance involved a Syrian Phoenician woman who came to Him on behalf of her daughter, asking Jesus to cast a demon out of her. At first Jesus was reluctant to grant her request, because His mission was specifically to the Jews, but as she persisted He said:

"you may go; the demon has left your daughter."

She went home and found her child lying on the bed, and the demon gone.

(Mark 7: 24-30)

It is significant that Matthew's account of this miracle, which amplifies the event, further states that Jesus also said to the woman:

"Woman, you have great faith! Your request is granted."

(Matt. 15: 28)

So we see that in all three cases, the petitioners did not come to Jesus only with a request; they were extremely concerned for the sick one, with real love, determination and faith in Jesus' power to grant their request across the miles. We are thus in the realm of vicarious faith – the petitioners' faith in Jesus was really on behalf of the ones who were sick. They were not merely making requests; they believed that once Jesus expressed His willingness to heal, then the miracle would take place. This is a vital lesson for us to learn today.

On account of these Biblical instances I have taught that although it is the norm for sick people to receive direct ministry from Anne and myself in the Name of Jesus, yet it is right for us to encourage Christians to come to Jesus on behalf of sick relatives and friends for whom they are deeply concerned, and to believe that He only has to speak the word of healing from His heavenly throne, and their loved ones will be healed. So we have taught petitioners not only to pray to Jesus for loved ones, but to **believe** for a miracle.

To this end we brought into being an Intercessors' Fellowship to go alongside our ministry to the sick. It was led, until her retirement, by Mrs Stella Godsmark, who lives at Spilsby. We had about forty intercessors to whom she sent prayer requests, giving them as much detail as possible about each sufferer, including age, sex, address, and especially informing them about as much as was known of each sick person's condition and need.

Stella split the Fellowship into groups so that no one would have too many folk for whom to intercede, but could concentrate on a few. She urged the intercessors to engage in believing prayer and to have real faith in God for victorious answers. She regularly encouraged them by sending out testimonies to the answers to their faith, and always sent me a copy in response to the prayer-requests I had sent her. It is difficult to exaggerate the number of the miracles that happened all over the nation in answer to our Fellowship's faith-full petitions. These included healings of or provision for:

- cancer
- broken bones
- broken relationships
- the salvation of loved ones
- depression
- phobias
- chest conditions
- pain

- ♦ jobs for unemployed folk
- ♦ new homes
- ♦ blood pressure
- ♦ organic illness

and so on to include just about every imaginable need. Stella had a remarkable, God-given calling and effectiveness in this ministry.

When I was vicar at St Paul's, Hainault, 1970-75, we had very powerful Praise & Gospel Healing Services every Tuesday evening. Every week the church was packed to capacity. We actually encouraged people to send in prayer requests, which we, together with the faith-filled congregation, brought before the Lord at 10.00 pm each Tuesday. We had asked petitioners to sit quietly and spiritually "tune in with us" in their homes at this time. Again, every week we were able to report to our congregation wonderful miracles performed by Jesus in answer to our faith.

Since 1975, except for two years pastoring St Luke's Episcopal Church, Seattle, USA, Anne and I have had no church base for our ministry. We have been entirely engaged in itinerant work, mainly at public meetings. Stella Godsmark's retirement from her work as secretary and organiser of the Intercessors' Fellowship resulted in the work never really getting off the ground since that time. However, Anne and I have still felt a burden to give people at meetings the opportunity to bring their needy but absent loved ones to the Lord. I have done this by asking those who desired to be involved in this spiritual act of faith, to stand and in silence think about and also picture these absent folk in real love and to sympathise (suffer with) with the ones they have on their hearts. After a little while I ask them to turn their thoughts to Jesus and visualise Him on His throne in glory. I have reminded them that He said, after His resurrection, "All authority in heaven and on earth has been given to me." (Matt. 28) Then I have suggested that they speak aloud the name of their loved one to Him. I wait a while, then I say, "On the count of three shout out the Name 'Jesus' and believe for a miracle across the miles." The cry has often echoed around the building. After this I urge them to praise the Lord in anticipation of good news. The results of this act of faith have come back to us by the score.

In Finland relatives had been urgently called to the hospital where their loved one was nearing the end with terminal cancer. They had gone to be with her when she died. However, miles away in Helsinki, another relative had taken a different course. She was standing in one of our meetings, believing Jesus for a miracle. The critically ill woman began to make an astonishing and rapid recovery. When we met Finnish friends later at a conference, they told us that the woman is now living a normal life, with no trace of cancer in her body.

On another occasion, in Ireland, I was given rather a shock during this ministry. As I was uttering the words about the healing of the absent sick, one intercessor suddenly fell with a tremendous crash onto the stone floor of the church. Angels must have hurried to put an invisible cushion under her, for she was not hurt. Her friend, however, was **healed**. Florence later wrote:

"As I stood in the prayer line, thinking of her and what Jesus can do, the Lord touched me, and I fell down with a terrible bang in the Spirit. Well, since then, she has phoned to say that the bleeding has stopped and she hasn't taken a tablet since. We have praised the Lord in tears and laughter."

In this ministry the Lord has overcome all language barriers. He **had** to do so when we were in Spain. A remarkable miracle resulted. It involved a very sick woman on the other side of the country who didn't even know that faith was being exercised on her behalf at a meeting we were holding in a believer's house.

I learned the next day that this very sick woman just couldn't understand what was happening to her as she lay in bed. All she knew was that at about 10.00 pm she began to feel very much better. She could hardly believe it, but as strength flowed into her body and new life into her limbs, she decided to see if she could get out of bed. She easily succeeded, and was discovered, early in the morning, to be doing her housework – for the first time in ten years! Excited relatives asked us if we could go and visit her. We did so, and told her that it was Jesus who had made her whole.

Sometimes believers have actually asked me, during a prayer time for the absent sick, to **minister** to them as they have believed for an absent sick person who was on their heart. One woman wrote:

"About eleven years ago I went to a Service in the Millmead Centre at Guildford where you were speaking. My friend was ill, she was expecting her fourth child and had been very sick for five months. She was weak and in bed most of the time. I came forward for prayer on her behalf. That night her sickness stopped, she became stronger and a normal healthy son 'Danny' was born."

His parents became Christians through this experience.

One final way in which God brings healing to the absent sick remains to be discussed. This is the way in which believers can take prayer cloths which have been prayed over by a Spirit-anointed minister of God to a sick loved one, to be used as yet another 'point of contact' between the healing power of God and the afflicted person. This ministry is based on the account in Acts (Chapter 19) which reads:

> God did extraordinary miracles through Paul. Handker-
> chiefs and aprons that had touched him were taken to the
> sick and their illnesses were cured and the evil spirits left
> them.
>
> (verses 11-12)

We have not particularly promulgated this ministry, but when asked to do so, have prayed over handkerchiefs or pieces of cloth at the request of believers, and we have received testimony to some "extraordinary" miracles.

One or two typical letters are:

- "I feel I must write. I've been an arthritic for a number of years, with other troubles. Now I have received a tremendous improvement over the last few weeks after receiving a prayer-cloth. Now the fear of being alone that I have suffered the last twelve months has gone!"

- "Just to thank you for the prayer cloth that you kindly sent. I am glad to say that the ulcer in my left leg has been healed."

- "I wrote to you about my mother Mrs Xigi, who lives in Greece and was suffering from cancer. I sent her the prayer cloth you sent me and I am happy to tell you that by the grace of the Lord she is better. The lump has completely gone."

- "I have to testify to healing and help we have been receiving through prayer, belief and the use of the prayer handkerchief. My wife's blood pressure continues to be normal."

So, by one means or another we have seen that it is God's perfect will to heal physical afflictions, even of those who cannot receive direct, personal ministry and we are without doubt that He does so.

PART SIX

Healing by Deliverance
from Demons

Chapter 23
The nature of demonic sickness

In our Biblical studies we saw that God created other beings than humans and that they inhabit the heavenly spheres. We saw that Lucifer, an archangel, fell from grace and took legions of angels with him into rebellion against God. We saw also that he has established a rival kingdom to that of our Heavenly Father and that this will only finally be overthrown at the glorious return of our Lord Jesus Christ. It now remains for me to add to this teaching that the realm of the occult, which we saw (page 42) is a forbidden religion for God's people in both the Old Testament and the New, is his domain, and that Christians dabble in it at their peril.

In our previous studies we saw that the devil's angels are called demons or unclean spirits (these are taught as identical evil forces in Revelation Chapter 16: 13-14) and that they can, as seen in the ministry of Jesus, cause all manner of sicknesses of the body and soul. The question remains to be asked as to how these demons gain access to the human spirit, soul and body. The answer to that, in the Bible's teaching and the experience of the Church, is that this is through occult involvement or grievous, repetitive sin.

The occult realm is very wide and deep and, as we have seen (page 8), all engagement with spiritists such as mediums, fortune tellers, clairvoyants, necromancers and diviners can bring a person into satanic bondage, causing sickness of the body, disturbances in the soul and a sense of the loss of a relationship with God. So Christians must ask themselves, or be asked by a counsellor, the following questions:

● Are you aware that you yourself, either of your parents or any grandparent was involved in spiritism or any occult practices?
● Are you aware that any other relative or person that you have had close contact with at any time was similarly involved?
● Have you ever been aware of "voices" speaking to you in your mind?
● Do you feel that you are "psychic" in any way, such as sometimes being made aware of future events?
● Have you ever read:
> books on reincarnation?
> books on pagan religions claiming their "deity" to be God instead of acknowledging Christ as the only way to God?
> books on metaphysics?
> books on mind science?
> your horoscope, or have had it read to you?
> books on spiritualism or magic?
● Have you ever attended any spiritist seance or tried to contact any dead person?
● Have you seen seances in films at the cinema or on TV?
● Have you played with a ouija board or Tarot cards for guidance or even for fun?
● Have you used or used others in water divining?
● Have you had your fortune told?

> Other areas to question are:
> mental telepathy
> clairvoyance
> casting spells
> using a divining rod or pendulum – even a wedding ring, swinging it to predict the sex of an unborn child

table tipping
levitation
Astral travel
automatic writing
modern rock and pop music
using the help of a psychic healer
superstitions – such as touching wood, wishing on a star, a black cat, Friday 13th, throwing salt over your shoulder, etc

Have you looked at any pornographic literature or films?

Have you committed yourself to any secret society or masonic order?

Have you ever been under the influence of alcohol, like being "merry" or drunk?

Have you taken "hard" non-prescription drugs such as heroin?

Have you engaged in or belonged to any cults or false religions such as Theosophy, "Church of Latter-Day Saints" (Mormons), Jehovah's Witnesses, Christian Science, Scientology, Yoga, transcendental meditation, Eastern meditation, spiritist church, or any cult that believes in reincarnation?

Have you engaged in any role play games which have psychic or occult connotations and characters?

And then **have you engaged in flagrant sexual sin such as adultery or fornication, homosexual or lesbian practices**?

If you have done any of these things, then you have been involved in the devil's realm, and this could cause you all kinds of sickness of spirit, soul and body; for even in these days "the devil prowls around like a roaring lion looking for someone to devour" (1 Peter 5: 8). He is, in my experience, a master of camouflage and can even appear as an "angel of light". We need to "resist him, standing firm in the faith" (1 Peter 5: 9).

It must be stated that there are, in fact, various depths of satanic assault on people's lives, even those of Christians. There are "*temptations*" which come from the devil. These even Jesus could not avoid (Matt. Chap. 4) and are inevitable in our lives on this earth. We have, however, no reason to give in to these and fall into sin. We must, when tempted, cast ourselves on the grace of God and so have victory in this realm, being strengthened by Him and even becoming mature in our Christian lives.

Or we may be *harassed* by evil spirits, or even *tormented* by them, even as Christians. I have known people also to be *oppressed* by them and so feel fearful and insecure, or even depressed. The most serious state we can be in is to "have a demon" or be "ruled" by a spirit – or, in common language, "be possessed". In the case of harassment, torment, and oppression the unclean spirit, or demon, is still outside of us. However, if we are "demonised", or possessed, then the evil force has actually entered our spirit, soul and body and has, at least in certain areas, taken control of us and we are in real need of help.

Finally in this study, it needs to be said that we can come under bondage to evil forces through having been solemnly *cursed* by literally anyone, but especially by witches, warlocks, gypsies or other psychics, and this can cause us to be sick in any part of our being. Paul writes in Ephesians – to Christians in all ages:

Finally, be strong in the Lord and in His mighty power.

Put on the full armour of God so that you can take your stand against the devil's schemes.

For our struggle is not against flesh and blood, but against the rulers, against the authorities, against the powers of this dark world and against the spiritual forces of evil in the heavenly realms.

Therefore put on the full armour of God, so that when the day of evil comes, you may be able to stand your ground, and after you have done everything, to stand.

(Eph. 6: 10-13)

Chapter 24
Personal spiritual warfare

If anyone, especially a Christian, has either deliberately or inadvertently been involved in the occult or flagrant, repeated sin, and thereby come under satanic bondage in spirit, soul and/or body, then they themselves can take steps to re-establish their wholeness in Christ.

Firstly, there must be a readiness to admit such involvement and to face it openly, frankly and square-on. It is very helpful to do this by admitting it to a Christian minister, friend or counsellor.

Secondly, there has to be a complete, utter and absolute **renunciation** of the involvement in this sin. This may well entail burning books, destroying films or videos, breaking off relationships, leaving cults or secret societies, and cleansing one's home of ornaments, occult or pagan objects and the like. Anything and everything involved with the past sin must unreservedly be destroyed and go into the rubbish tip.

Thirdly, there must be a **confession** of the involvement to the Lord with real repentance from the heart. This must be followed by a claiming of God's forgiveness through His sacrifice for sin on Calvary. The believer can have confidence that he or she has been completely cleansed from all sin through faith in the Lord Jesus Christ.

Fourthly, it is a very wise step to engage the help of a Spirit-filled Christian to cut the spiritual umbilical cord through which Satan has afflicted us from past generations. Such a believer can also help in the breaking of the power of curses which have been put on the sufferer, by taking authority and breaking all curses on one's life, such as poverty, sickness, and death. All curses on marriage, family, children and relationships can also be likewise broken, together with curses of rejection, pride, rebellion, lust, incest, rape, fear, insanity or confusion. Curses which have caused one's sexual life, emotions and habits to be sinful can similarly be broken. We can also, together with others, bind the "god of this world" who has blinded the eyes of our unbelieving relatives and friends to the light of the glorious Gospel of Jesus Christ, and so render them free to accept it (2 Cor. 4: 4; Mark 4: 15).

It is important during all this spiritual activity that we also forgive any person, living or dead, who has in any way sinned against us, or spoiled our lives. The renunciation that we express must also be by a definite act of our whole being, especially of our will, as we "Renounce the devil and all his works, the pomp and glory of the world, and the sinful desires of the flesh" (1662 Book of Common Prayer).

The Bible teaches that God has given every Christian weapons with which effectively to wage spiritual warfare for our continuing wholeness and protection against the enemy, the Prince of Darkness. Paul writes to the Church at Corinth:

> *The weapons we fight with are not the weapons of the world. On the contrary, they have divine power to demolish strongholds.*

> (2 Cor. 10: 4)

There are six such weapons which I have found to be powerful in this way in my own life and ministry.

Firstly, we must be **aware of the power** that dwells within us, especially through the baptism in the Holy Spirit. Jesus promised His followers, just before His ascension, such an earth and heaven shaking power (Acts of the Apostles Chapter 1: 5-8) and they received it on the Day of Pentecost (Acts 2: 1-4). Paul urges all Christians to "be filled with the Spirit" (Eph. 5: 18) and when we are so filled we have unimaginable ability to wage spiritual warfare.

Secondly, we must learn to **use the authority** given to Christians in the Name of Jesus. Our Lord Jesus has supreme authority over all spiritual forces on earth and in heaven, and as we have seen (page 16) He has delegated that authority to His people to use on their Christian pilgrimage. So we can **command** all the forces of darkness to go from our lives in His Name. (1 Cor. 15: 24; 1 Pet. 3: 22; Luke 10: 17,19). We have the power to bind these evil forces and render them helpless (Matt. 16: 19).

Thirdly, we can **plead the blood of the Lamb** against evil forces. Jesus taught that He was shedding His blood to bring His people into a New Covenant relationship with God (Matt. 26: 28; Luke 22: 20). Within that Covenant the Blood cleanses us from all sin: the handle in our lives which the devil uses to swing us around (1 John 1: 7; Rev. 1: 5). Furthermore, His blood was shed on Calvary at Passover time and there is therefore a link between Jesus' blood and the blood which the Hebrews used in Egypt to protect them from the angel of death (Exodus Chap. 12). As one old chorus says of Christians, "I'm going to keep right under the Blood where the devil can do me no harm."

Fourthly, to keep free from demonic sickness, or to cure it, we must **engage in the power of prayer**. We can pray with our understanding, and Jesus has promised to give us whatever we ask in His Name (John 16: 23-26). He is always interceding for us and for our wholeness (Rom. 8: 27-34; Heb. 7: 25) and when we pray in the Spirit, with "groanings which cannot be uttered" (Rom. 8: 26 *NASV*) we are using a very powerful weapon against the devil and his minions.

168

Fifthly, we must **confess God's word**. This, Paul calls in Ephesians, "the sword of the Spirit" (Eph. 6: 17). Jesus, when tempted by the devil in the desert, quoted God's word to get the victory over him (Matt. 4). We must do the same when assailed by the enemy who will, at times, try to deceive us and tell us all manner of lies about ourselves, God, or others.

Finally, as our sixth weapon in the face of enemy attacks we must **lift up our voice in praise**. Jehoshaphat commanded his people to do this, as recorded in the Old Testament, and won a victory against all the odds as the enemy fled (2 Chron. 20: 20-22). Paul and Silas praised God when they were held in chains with their feet in the stocks, and suddenly the prison doors were opened and their chains loosened (Acts 16: 25-26). So our chains, with which Satan has bound us, will fall away, and even the prison of depression in which he has trapped us will open to the light of God's joy and peace when in the face of the enemy we praise the Lord (see Ps. 126: 2; Ps. 150; 2 Sam. 6: 14; Ps. 95; Acts 10: 46, and, for the shout of victory, Joshua 6: 16).

So the Lord has given us means whereby we ourselves can personally do battle with our spiritual enemy and, when brought into bondage, set ourselves free; when assailed by the devil in any way, surely win the victory and remain whole in spirit, soul and body; and through the conflict we may even grow into spiritual maturity and wholeness.

Chapter 25
Deliverance from evil forces

Although we are able, with the weapons of warfare which God has given us, to keep ourselves free from the inroads of satanic influence in our spirits, souls and bodies, yet in my experience, Christians who are being severely assailed by the enemy often need the outside help of a Spirit-filled minister to drive away the powers of evil or to break the bondage of curses. There is no admission of weakness in seeking such ministry, for God has made us inter-dependent in our Christian pilgrimage on earth. This is especially so in the case of those who have become demonised or ruled by an evil spirit. Such "possession" plays havoc with the wholeness of our spirits, souls and bodies.

To engage in this spiritual deliverance the minister has to have the ability to 'discern' (1 Cor. 12: 10) the presence of the evil spirit in the life of the afflicted person and to know what sort of spirit it is; for example, a 'spirit of lust', a 'spirit of fear', a 'spirit of death' and so on. He must have not the slightest fear of these evil forces and must be absolutely confident about the authority he has, in the Name of Jesus, to cast the spirit out of the afflicted person's life.

God promised that the seed of a woman would bruise Satan's head (Gen. 3: 15) and the New Testament is unequivocal in its declaration that "The reason the Son of God appeared was to destroy the devil's work" (1 John 3: 8) and that He is above and has power over all Satan's domain (Col. 2: 10; 2: 15; Phil. 2: 10; Eph. 1: 18-23). The New Testament also teaches that the Lord has established an army of those who are born again (1 Pet. 1: 1-8), baptised in the Holy Spirit, transferred from the kingdom of darkness into the Kingdom of Light (Col. 1: 12-14) and are given power and authority, delegated to them by Jesus Christ, to cast out and defeat Satan's minions (Luke 9: 1-2; Mark 16: 14-20; Acts 13: 4-12; Acts 8; Heb. 2: 5-8; 2 Tim. 2: 12; 1 Cor. 6: 2-3; Rom. 8: 17). The Church is therefore commissioned by Him to do this (Acts 5: 16; Ch. 16: 16-18). The authority the minister of deliverance has is in the Name of Jesus (Acts 16: 18). The offending evil spirit is first 'bound', and thus rendered helpless, and then it is cast into the pit in chains to await the judgement of Christ.

I was myself launched into this ministry by being attacked by a witch when I was vicar of St Paul's, Hainault, 1970-75 (see my book *It's True!* for a full account of this event), and have been very much engaged in the ministry of deliverance ever since. I have never laid hands on a demonised person (although Jesus did on one occasion at least [Luke 13]), I have never used holy water, communion wine or any other material thing. I have always cast out evil spirits purely by the use of an authoritative command "in the Name of Jesus", and I believe that this is meant to be the normal and proper New Testament way of dealing with these entities.

I have already written about some dramatic examples of the results of my deliverance ministry and how, in the name of Jesus, it has brought peace and wholeness to afflicted people (see *It's True!*), but I will add a few further instances to illustrate the power of this form of healing.

Once I was taking a meeting in the Midlands in a large church when we were interrupted by the terrible noise of furniture being smashed at the rear of the church. A young man was, in fact, picking up chairs and crashing them one against the other. The minister and stewards tried to restrain him by pinning him to the floor. But he shook them off with supernatural strength and ran from the building. Immediately I urged the congregation to pray.

"Destructive spirit, I bind you," I declared across the distance, "you shall not hurt him any more. In the Name of Jesus, I loose him from your control."

We then prayed that the Spirit of God would direct his feet back to the church.

Surely enough, he returned, and I discovered that he had been deeply involved in the meditational exercises of yoga. This had obviously been the point of the spirit's entry.

"I felt my body was going one way, despite all my mind wanted to do. I was taken over by something that used my body," he nervously explained.

It was all over in two minutes. He renounced the practice from his heart and, at the word of command, yet another spirit was despatched to the pit to await the judgement of Christ.

A woman wrote:

"After you had ministered to me, I could have skipped and danced back to my seat (after all for forty years these dreadful demons have had me in their power). I felt so light and free that I could hardly control my feet from dancing. Then came the acid test: coming home to the house where so much hate has been. I lifted my heart to God and went indoors believing He had done it. And He had, Brother Trevor, He had."

Perhaps one of the most unusual cases I ever had, which proved the power of the spoken word of command, concerned a young man classified as schizophrenic. He had lapsed into this state after losing his job and feeling unable to support his pretty wife and two young children. He had entered so deeply into a world of his own that he could not be reached by normal conversation. It was his wife who first sought my help, and I persuaded her to bring him along to my meeting in Hadleigh, Essex, whatever his condition.

The situation did not look very promising because at the beginning of the service he was just wandering about mumbling incoherently to himself. I went up to him but could obtain no rational replies to my questions. However, I took authority and commanded all evil spirits to leave his life. Immediately he became coherent. I kept in touch with him subsequently and discovered that all his mental problems had been healed.

Another man wrote:

> "The service changed my life. When my turn for healing came, I prayed, 'If you are really there, God, help me now.' As my eyes opened my body seemed filled with something wonderful, and, as I lay on the floor of the church I could see the altar cross shining. I rose up feeling I was walking on air. From that day my depression lifted. I renounced spiritism, became a Christian and every aspect of my life has changed."

M. Wardles:

> "I should say by God, through the meeting I believe I was delivered from something awful which has tormented me for many years. I have attempted suicide seven times, the last time being in March this year – all serious attempts. All this is over. I will give testimony if you think it is appropriate."

My wife, Anne, does not regard herself as having a deliverance ministry and usually leaves these cases to me. However, at Birmingham Christian Centre she was called upon to minister alone, in the vestry, to a young man who was having several epileptic fits every day. He was so likely to have a fit that he had to come to the church by taxi. Anne discerned that his problem was caused by a demon, and she commanded it to leave him. He went home by bus; soon went on a holiday by himself, and the last we heard he had had no more epileptic fits.

Recently I was called upon to minister to a young married man who loved the Lord but was absolutely addicted to pornographic books, magazines and films. He was constantly having sexual relations with prostitutes. He said that he just couldn't help it. His patient Christian wife was almost beside herself with the trouble caused and felt she could no longer tolerate being married to him. I cast out a demon and he catapulted backwards two or three yards as the evil force left him. He has, after a battle with temptation, been free ever since. His troubles, he told me afterwards, began with his almost inadvertently reading a pornographic magazine.

Follow-up of those delivered from evil spirits is very important, and they need the loving support of caring, Spirit-filled Christians. It is vitally important that the spiritual vacuum in their lives is filled by the Holy Spirit, otherwise, as Jesus taught, more spirits worse than the first will come in and fill it (Luke 11: 24-26).

Deliverance ministry, in my experience, need not be prolonged or need to be constantly repeated if the afflicted person subsequently puts their complete trust in Jesus Christ as Saviour and Lord and is filled with the Holy Spirit, engaging in deep Christian fellowship. Deliverance ministry brings wholeness to spirit, soul and body.

Chapter 26
Spiritual warfare and the Church

It is important that we see the total healing of the whole person through protection, ministry and spiritual warfare as set within the context of the fellowship of the Church.

We need to understand that God's special people have a new status in the spiritual realm. Together they share a position of reigning with Christ (Eph. 2: 4-6), "blessed . . . in the heavenly realms with every spiritual blessing" in Christ Jesus (Eph. 1: 3). They now sit with Christ in heavenly places. He has made them worthy to share all the treasures of those who belong to the kingdom of light (Rom. 8: 17; Eph. 1: 18-19; 2: 19). God has rescued them out of the darkness and gloom of Satan's domain and brought them into the kingdom of his dear Son (Col.1:12-13; 3:1-4). In this position of privilege they have a unique place of protection. For them the promise holds true.

We who dwell "in the shelter of the Most High" and abide "in the shadow of the Almighty, will say to the Lord, 'My refuge and my fortress: my God, in whom I trust'" (Psalm 91:1-2). God is our refuge and strength, a rock and a fortress against the attacks of the enemy (Psalm 31).

Little wonder a New Testament writer confidently declared that overwhelming victory is ours through Christ. Nothing can ever separate us from God's love (Rom. 8: 38-39). This spiritual security is for both mature Christians and their children. Believers, "little ones", stand under the protecting umbrella of the faith of their parents and of the whole Church. Eventually, however, in order to enter fully into their heritage, the "little ones" also must experience the new birth. God has no grandchildren.

This place of privilege which Christians enjoy does not mean that they will never be exposed to Satan's assaults upon their souls. The evidence of the Bible, history and personal experience show Christians still will be tempted. Because they are God's people, rowing against the tide of evil in the world, they will experience more temptation than unbelievers can ever know. The advice given to them in this situation is to "Resist the devil and he will flee from you" (Jas. 4: 7). Yes, Christians will be tempted but they have no need to be overwhelmed (Heb. 2: 18).

Christians will also be persecuted. During Satan's earliest assaults upon the Church Peter wrote: "Your adversary the devil prowls around like a roaring lion, seeking someone to devour. Resist him, firm in your faith" (1 Pet. 5: 8-10). Jesus forewarned His disciples that they would be persecuted and He actually told them to rejoice in their sufferings, recognising them as a mark of good spiritual pedigree (Matt. 5: 10-12).

God apparently allows His special people periodically to be persecuted in order to test and purify their faith (1 Pet. 1: 6-8). The Bible teaches that even though the devil may thrust Christians into prison and slay them, they will be vindicated in the end by their heavenly Father (Rev. 2: 10).

Christians may even experience a "hammering" from Satan. Paul knew this experience when he complained about "a thorn . . . in the flesh, a messenger of Satan, to harass me". He was really brought low, and three times he pleaded with God to get rid of it. The Lord's reply to him is of abiding significance for all Christians: "My grace is sufficient for you, for my power is made perfect in weakness" (2 Cor. 12: 7-9).

God has provided His people with a spiritual armour with which to ward off Satan's attacks. If we wear it we shall still be found standing even when the devil has done all he can to hurt us. The armour is the belt of truthfulness, the breastplate of right living, shoes to facilitate speed in preaching the gospel of peace, the shield of faith with which we can stop all flaming arrows of the evil one, the helmet of salvation and the sword of the Spirit (the words God has spoken) (Eph. 6: 13-17). This, of course, is a picture of a Roman soldier in battle dress. It is also a picture of a Christian squaring up to the legions of the devil. The people of God are like soldiers in an army, a theme taken up in many battle-cry hymns:

> Onward, Christian soldiers, marching as to war,
> With the cross of Jesus going on before.
>
> (S. Baring-Gould)

The words of this hymn pulsate with meaning and significance when one's eyes are wide open to the reality of spiritual warfare. Christians are called to fight a battle in which they know they can never ultimately be defeated. Christ is risen!

As we set out to engage in this conflict, it is of vital importance to realise that we are not involved simply in one-armed combat. It was to the Church, the new generation people collectively, that Jesus promised, "On this rock I will build my church, and the powers of death (hell) shall not prevail against it" (Matt. 16: 18).

Christians cover and protect each other by their mutual faith. It is true that in this battle, "Together we stand, divided we fall". The Church is more like a Roman turtle than a conglomeration of solitary soldiers. The turtle was a battalion of soldiers standing side by side, back to back, shield to shield until they were a massive wall of metal – a human tank. Those in the middle turned their shields to face upwards, providing a metal roof to protect against arrows from the sky. Thus formed, this solid metal mass would move steadily towards objectives in enemy territory, invincible in their complete solidarity.

Christians, too, must join together in unity, forming "prayer turtles" and cutting across denominational lines in every place where the spiritual battle is raging.

The words of the hymn writer must always be a reality: "Like a mighty army moves the Church of God," as we steadily march against the positions the enemy now occupies, both in the world and the human heart.

Opposing an offensive such as this, Satan's tactics are always to divide the Church, to set one Christian against another, to stir leaders into party strife, to cause heresies and schisms. We experienced this strategy of the enemy when I was a vicar of St Paul's Church, Hainault, London, as we moved out into spiritual warfare. Satan even sent false prophets among us to cause confusion and division. Christians who, by their words and deeds, divide the Church, are acting as Satan's emissaries (Matt. 7: 15-23). Drastic disciplinary action must be taken against them (l Cor. 5: 5). They might even have to be expelled in order to preserve the vital unity of God's people (Titus 3: 10).

It follows from the picture of the turtle that the Church, the turtle of God's true people, is a place of real protection from the ravages of Satan. Add to this the Lord's promises to His people and the knowledge we have of His victory and surely no Christian, in deep involvement with others, needs to be afraid of the devil and all his works. Unfortunately, I have met many frightened Christians in my ministry. This is sad because fear, the opposite of faith, is a serious loophole in our defences. Once a Christian becomes afraid he is very vulnerable to Satan's power.

This was so in the case of three Christians who telephoned my vicarage in abject terror. My wife, Anne, answered the call and was told, "We have just passed a house where a seance was in progress. A great black cloud

178

seemed to come out of the door and envelop us." The young man reporting the incident was in such terror that he could hardly get his breath. Anne could hear his teeth chattering. "Ask Trevor to come immediately to give us deliverance," came the urgent plea. My wife explained to them their standing in Christ. She told them that they could claim the victory which was theirs in the name of Jesus.

"Go back," she said, "and tell all the evil to go from your friends and from the area in the name of Jesus. We will be praying for you."

A few minutes later the young Christians phoned again, shouting with delight, "It worked! It worked! Praise the Lord!"

On another occasion a Christian wrote to me along the following lines: "I am very frightened. I have recently moved into a new flat and have discovered that the people below are holding seances. I feel strange tremblings coming over me and cannot sleep."

I explained to my correspondent the authority all Christians have through faith in Jesus. Then I added, "I hope to hear soon from a medium saying, 'Please help me. A Christian is praying above me and I can't get through to the occult.'"

So often Christians seeking help have simply been frightened. They have been fearful of places or of people involved in the occult. The devil's power over them has been directly in proportion to the extent to which they have feared him. Christians who resist him find that he soon flees.

An old Chinese fable can illustrate this truth. It is said that once upon a time a town was being harassed by a terrible dragon. The more the townsfolk fled from it, the larger it grew until it became as large as a mountain. One day a boy, armed only with a stick, came to town, and to the amazement of the folk volunteered to kill the dragon. He had realised the secret of victory and set out with confidence. Eventually he returned with the news that the dragon was dead. How had he killed it? He had simply walked closer and closer towards the enemy, completely unafraid. As he did so it grew smaller and smaller until he was able to pick it up, put it in the palm of his hand and kill it with his stick. Shades of David and Goliath? That in principle demonstrates how we should be aware of our authority and victory in Jesus Christ, and points the way to deal with the devil.

Christians who treat the devil in this way are secure from his ravages. They are secure but not immune. It is a sad fact that sometimes Christians do let Satan influence them to such an extent that he is able to overcome their solitary defences and enter into them. This was true of Ananias and his wife Sapphira in the early Church. They undoubtedly were members of the early Christian community, yet they took themselves out of turtle formation when they agreed together to cheat the Church. Peter had to ask them, "How is it that Satan has so filled your heart that you have lied to the Holy Spirit . . . ?" Their end was disastrous (Acts 5: 1-11).

It seems that in the case of Galatia, the devil was actually able to gain control, not merely over individuals but over a whole church. Paul wrote, "You foolish Galatians! Who has bewitched you? Before your very eyes Jesus Christ was clearly portrayed as crucified." (Gal. 3: 1). Other New Testament writings also reveal that some of the early Christians succumbed to deceiving spirits and things taught by demons (1 Tim. 4: 1).

In every case I have known of genuine possession-problems in believers, there has always been a definite, traceable reason why they have become so very troubled. Sometimes they have actually had fellowship with demons by engaging in the occult, either before or after conversion (1 Cor. 10: 20-21). Other ways I have known Satan to gain a hold on believers are:

1. Inadequate renunciation of sin.
2. Prolonged sinful disobedience to Christ.
3. Engagement in sexual perversions and pornography
4. The continual use of hard drugs.
5. Rebellion against Jesus.
6. Failure to yield every area of life to Christ.
(This leaves Satan in control of some territory in the soul)
7. Straying back into the world.
8. Constant indulgence in bad temper or violence.
9. Involvement in the occult.

In most cases of such failures in the Christian life, deep repentance, renunciation, confession and faith in God's forgiving love are sufficient to restore the penitent. However, sometimes where Satan has definitely used the Christian's weakness to re-establish his rule, deliverance ministry has been necessary. Only then has the Christian been restored to fellowship and begun to enjoy the victorious life of the people of God.

This victorious life, triumphing in the face of overwhelming spiritual odds, is possible only for God's special people. They alone can stand against the onslaught of the devil. They know that they can win through, because of the victory of their Saviour Jesus. He has defeated all the forces of wickedness and now has a status high above all rule and authority and every name that can be named, not only in this world but also in the next (Eph. 1: 15-23).

True believers cannot afford to become too preoccupied with Satan's power because they know its boundaries and its limits. They are a people who continually fix their minds on the Lord Jesus Christ. They know that the God of all power and might, the author and giver of all good things, and to whom they belong, will defend them from all evil that may assail body, mind or spirit. The Lord's Prayer, "Lead us not into temptation, but deliver us from evil" (Matt. 6: 13), is continually answered by God who is their refuge and strength. They are well aware that Satan can ravage the world of men which has given itself to him. They also know that everything the devil does to tempt, assail, harm or overwhelm faithful Christians will be completely reversed for their good.

Satan, in the end, can only further God's purposes for His people. Satan is a defeated foe. Jesus has triumphed (Phil. 2: 9-11). This is the news that the new generation people should proclaim to the ends of the earth until Jesus returns to establish His glorious Kingdom.

PART SEVEN

Wholeness and the
outward-directed life

Chapter 27
Wholeness and the life of service

It remains in our study of total healing wrought by God in the human spirit, soul and body, to point out that in seeking such healing we can be far too introspective: concerned only with ourselves; our sickness; our need for peace; our need to be free from sin and guilt. In the final part of this book I shall point outwardly to the practical Christian life lived within and from the Church.

Such an outward-flowing life, deeply knit in Christian fellowship, is in itself extremely therapeutic, and it is the fellowship of the Church that the New Testament portrays as the context within which we are healed. This total healing is in turn manifested in the life we live in marriage, work, society and the world. It is firstly a life of service.

One of the lessons which our Lord was continually teaching His disciples was that "greatness" within the new People of God would lie in serving one another. This was, of course, a completely revolutionary concept and therefore He had to impress the idea upon them over and over again, as they continually argued amongst themselves about which of them would eventually be the greatest in the coming kingdom (Luke 9: 46). Jesus' teaching is seen for instance in the graphic way in which He took hold of a child and, placing him in the midst of them, stated that anyone who would be great in the kingdom of God would have, in fact, to become just like such a little child (Matt. 18: 1- 10). He spoke most directly about the greatest kind of service, however, when He said to His disciples:

> "You know that those who are regarded as rulers of the Gentiles lord it over them, and their high officials exercise authority over them. Not so with you. Instead, whoever wants to become great among you must be your servant;

185

and whoever wants to be first must be the slave of all. For
even the Son of Man did not come to be served, but to serve,
and to give his life as a ransom for many".

(Mark 10: 42-45)

The ultimate expression of this teaching is, of course, to be found in the act of Jesus when He washed His disciples' feet (John 13: 1-11). The party of thirteen had, at that time, arrived at the "upper room" which had been loaned to Jesus so that He might have somewhere to celebrate His Passover with His disciples.

Perhaps it was because of the necessary secrecy involved at that time that there were no servants present to perform the usual courtesies afforded to guests. These were especially that one of the lowest servants of the household would untie the guests' sandals; whilst the lowest servant of all would perform the most menial of tasks, that of actually washing the dust from the travellers" feet. One can imagine all the disciples passing the bowl of water, each being unwilling to adopt a more servile posture than his fellows. Who was going to be the one to admit that all the others were superior to him and do the foot-washing? We can imagine their astonishment when Jesus Himself took the towel and the bowl of water and began to wash His disciples' feet.

Peter felt such a sense of shame that he began to argue with Jesus, saying: "Lord, you shall never wash my feet." Jesus, however, knew that this would be His last opportunity to teach this impetuous man, and indeed all the others, the most important lesson they could ever learn to equip them for their future spiritual leadership, and so He went as far as saying, "If I do not wash you, you have no part with me." Peter succumbed, and he learned, along with all the others, the essential meaning of greatness and the true expression of a "whole" person, because only whole people can serve in this way.

It was when Jesus had washed each of the disciples' feet, and by so doing dealt a death blow to their pride and misguided ideas about being important, which pervade the sin-sick soul, that He could say to them:

"Now that I, your Lord and Teacher, have washed your feet, you also should wash one another's feet. I have set you an example, that you should do as I have done for you."

(John 13: 14-15)

The importance of this whole spirit of service within the Christian community can hardly be exaggerated. It made a deep impression on the minds of the first Christians and was reiterated many times by the apostles in their exhortations to the early churches as recorded in the epistles of the New Testament. Perhaps it is nowhere more completely stated than in St Paul's letter to the Philippians, where he urged the believers in that church to:

Let this mind be in you, which was also in Christ Jesus: Who, being in the form of God, thought it not robbery to be equal with God: But made himself of no reputation, and took upon him the form of a servant, and was made in the likeness of men: And being found in fashion as a man, he humbled himself, and became obedient unto death, even the death of the cross.

(Philippians 2: 5-8, *AV*)

It was for this reason also that St Peter urged all. Christians to be subject to one another, and be clothed with humility: for "God opposes the proud, but gives grace to the humble" (1 Pet. 5: 5).

It follows that all the gifts and ministries of the Holy Spirit which were outlined in previous chapters have to be seen in the light of this teaching: they are given so that those who receive them may serve the Christian

187

community, the Body of Christ in which God has placed them.

The customary word used therefore to describe the elders or the overseer of any church is correctly that of 'minister'. The reason is that it is the literal translation of the Greek word 'diakonos' or 'deacon', which means 'servant'. In this connection how well I remember my first bishop, the late John Ramsbotham, saying to me after ordaining me a 'priest' in the church of God, "Always remember, Trevor, that like me, the highest function you can ever perform in the Church is still that of a deacon. We are always called to minister; to serve the people of God."

When such an attitude prevails in the Church, then there can be no place for pride of position, or for the elders to "lord it over" the people under their jurisdiction. There can be no place for the pomp and ceremony which is, sadly, so often seen to surround church "dignitaries". The honour which will be accorded by the flock to their shepherds can never depend upon outward display, but will inevitably spring from the grateful hearts of those who feel that they are being truly served in the name and Spirit of Jesus, the great shepherd of the sheep.

Service within the Christian community is not, however, only a matter of church leaders ministering to their people, but of members who are whole enough to do so, serving each other. The spirit of ministering to one another has, I believe, been rediscovered by the Church in recent years through the renewing work of the Holy Spirit.

As itinerants, it has been thrilling for Anne and myself to see far fewer churches where the people are simply sitting around waiting to be ministered to by their leader. Sometimes the new spirit of mutual service has been manifested even by the way in which renewed churches have arranged their furniture. This simple act can be very symbolic of a particular church's concept of service.

For instance, leader-dominated ministry has been portrayed in the Church of England by row upon row of immovable pews, all facing the pulpit, the lectern and the altar. They graphically depict an immobile congregation, having fellowship with the back of each other's heads, all stoically sitting waiting for ministry from the leader. The same is also true of the church buildings used by Roman Catholic, Methodist, United Reformed, Baptist and even Pentecostal denominations. Thankfully, such buildings are in my experience slowly being transformed to depict the truth that every member is a minister, called to serve the rest of his/her community. In such church buildings, as far as ever possible, the 'renewal' has led to rearrangement of the seating and other important items of furniture to portray the life of a church where Christians are always being encouraged to minister to each other.

There is still another New Testament ministry besides that of the church leaders and the renewed church members. It is that of the itinerant who specialises in one or more particular area of ministry (Eph. 4). During the years since 1975 when my wife and I launched out on such a ministry, recognised and blessed by my bishop to serve the wider Church, we have grown ever increasingly to realise the need for a spirit of service to prevail in the hearts of all 'wandering' ministries. At first, I suppose, we felt rather insecure as we set out to live by faith, and so were eager to build up a mailing list of people who promised to support us by prayer and by giving financially. In a way which was hidden to us at the time, we were subtly endeavouring, wherever we went, to promote our own ministry and reputation! Thankfully though, however slowly, we began to see that this was not scripturally the right attitude at all.

Our only excuse for this mistake is that we saw the same attitude prevailing in other itinerants with whom we were having fellowship and to whom we looked for guidance. However, in recent years we have seen that although God does call certain people with special ministries, such as healing, to itinerate, nevertheless they are **called to serve the different churches** which they are invited by elders to visit. Their only motive should be to endeavour to build up the churches' life and ministry and never their own!

Since the time we saw this to be true, we have never ministered anywhere in the world except at the invitation of a particular church community or group of such churches. Further, we have always regarded ourselves as in submission to the elders who have called us, for the whole length of time of our visit. Consequently, we have been used by the Lord to give 'input' into many churches' life, for as long as the elders have felt that we were serving a useful purpose. After that we have always left the area free from any interference from ourselves.

It is our view that any concept of empire-building, establishing one's own ministry, or being the focal point of a "move of God", on the part of itinerant ministers is contrary to the spirit of servanthood which befits all Christian ministers. They are called by God to serve local churches. Occasionally they are of course called to establish new churches where they are needed, but they should not be going about to promote their own ministries. Anne and I are still pleased to have the prayer support of several hundreds of people who occasionally send unsolicited gifts of money to help us. However, we make it clear that Christians should, in the main, be giving to and serving the Christian community to which they belong. Nowadays, our main source of finance is a gift from the church which has called us to serve them. This coheres with the Biblical teaching of Jesus that a "labourer is worthy of his hire", and Paul's affirmation that those who minister to people in spiritual matters have a right to reap their material well-being (1 Cor. 9: 11-12).

In the New Testament, of course, the spirit of service is not only to be alive within the Christian community itself. The apostles teach that it should also be the attitude of Christian employers to their employees and vice-versa. So Paul writes:

> Slaves, obey your earthly masters with respect and fear, and with sincerity of heart, just as you would obey Christ. Obey them not only to win their favour when their eye is on you, but like slaves of Christ, doing the will of God from your heart. Serve wholeheartedly, as if you were serving the Lord, not men . . . And masters, treat your slaves in the same way.
>
> (Eph. 6: 5-9)

Both Paul and Peter also taught that the spirit of loving service should be the hallmark of Christian homes (Eph. 5: 22, 6: 4; 1 Pet. 3: 1-7). There is no doubt also that New Testament writers urged members of Christian communities to be model citizens of the state where they abode even if the rulers were not Christians. So Peter wrote:

> Submit yourselves for the Lord's sake to every authority instituted among men, whether to the king, as the supreme authority, or to governors, who are sent by him to punish those who do wrong and to commend those who do right. For it is God's will that by doing good you should silence the ignorant talk of foolish men. Live as free men, but do not use your freedom as a cover-up for evil; live as servants of God. Show proper respect to everyone: Love the brotherhood of believers, fear God, honour the king. (1 Pet. 2: 13-17)

191

(see also Rom. 13: 1-7)

Today, likewise, there can be no doubt that Christians, though primarily called to service within the Church, are also called by God to be examples of those who give service in a power-seeking world. As they are the epitome of service so, like the Christians of the New Testament period, they are following the supreme example of their Master.

One experiment in practical service to a local community in which I was privileged to participate was a community care scheme in which we, at the Spirit-filled Church of St Paul's, Hainault, felt it very important to be involved. We did this with other churches in the locality as an ecumenical venture. The scheme involved our having an "area warden" in every street in the locality. These were church members who visited all new people coming to live in their area, taking with them a brochure providing details of all the health, social, church, school and other facilities in the locality and offering any help needed.

These "wardens" also kept an eye on all the elderly, shut-in or other needy people resident near to them. If any need arose, they immediately phoned the scheme's administration officer, who had a long list of people in the churches who were able to offer such practical help as electrical, joinery or plumbing work or of people available in the daytime who were able to provide transport to hospitals etc. I was later involved in a similar scheme at St Luke's Episcopal Church in the Ballard area of Seattle. It was in such ways that we endeavoured, as churches, to serve the people in our area.

Perhaps the most important words in John's account of Jesus' very emotive occasion of foot washing, are that He performed this task in the full knowledge of who He actually was, where He came from and where He was going. In other words, Jesus could perform this task because He was perfectly secure within Himself and whole enough to do so. He knew His origin, His status and His destiny. He had nothing that He had to prove to Himself or others. Only when this is true of them, can His followers serve freely and lovingly within the Christian community, and outside in the world, without any sense of being inferior. Quite the reverse; they are the only people in the world who are truly free to follow His example.

Chapter 28
Wholeness and a life of love

St Paul, who in his letters to young churches had written so much about the duty of serving and giving within the Christian community, also stated that these and all other spiritual activities were worthless unless they were motivated by love. He did this especially in what has become the most well-known passage in all his writings (1 Cor. 13). Here he wrote:

> *If I give all I possess to the poor, and surrender my body to the flames, but have not love, I gain nothing. Love is patient, love is kind. It does not envy, it does not boast, it is not proud. or rude . . . And now these three remain: faith, hope, and love. But the greatest of these is love.*

(The whole chapter is a beautiful poem about love.)

St John, also, taught that love was always to be the predominant characteristic of the whole Christian within the Christian community. Love amongst the brethren is just as much a theme of his letters as God's love for man is of his Gospel. He constantly urges his readers to love one another with such words as:

> *We know that we have passed from death to life, because we love our brothers.*

> (l John 3: 14)

> *And this is his command: to believe in the name of his Son, Jesus Christ, and to love one another as he commanded us.*

> (1 John 3: 23)

> *Dear friends, let us love one another; for love comes from God. Everyone who loves has been born of God and knows God. Whoever does not love does not know God; because God is love .*

> (1 John 4: 7-8).

All is beautifully summed up in his statement:

> *And so we know and rely on the love God has for us. God is love. Whoever abides in love abides in God, and God abides in him.*
>
> (l John 4: 16)

The Greek word which John uses for 'love' is the beautiful word 'agapë', which indicates that Christians' love for each other when they are whole should never be based upon any self seeking (*Greek* 'eros'), nor simply be a matter of mutual goodwill (*Greek* 'philos'), but should emulate the love of Jesus Himself in His absolute sacrifice of self for the good of others (John 3: 16).

Once again, as with serving, it is interesting to note that in the New Testament epistles the object of Christian love was to be primarily other members of the Christian community. So in the writing of St Peter, the new Temple of God is made up of living stones, and these are to be cemented together by love. St Paul uses a different metaphor, but his teaching is the same when he likens the Church to a body, the members of which are to nurture each other in the wholeness of love, and so grow into the fullness of the stature of Christ (Eph. 4). Paul's collection of money from the Gentile churches, we note, was for the 'saints' who were in Jerusalem (Rom. 15: 26).

The gifts brought to the apostles by such men as Barnabas were also for distribution to other needy Christians (Acts 4: 34-37). Although, for us, the fact that such practical expressions of love were limited to other Christian brethren may seem to be an inadequate interpretation of Christian love, yet we must realise that it was a revolutionary concept for the people in the first century AD. It was this agapë love which was the hallmark of the Christian community.

It was the characteristic of love which also differentiated the New Covenant people of God from the Old.

No longer did they need to live according to a legalistic code and ritualistic system in order to be seen to be God's special people. Their relationship both to God and to each other was governed by the Law of Love, and it was this love that marked them out as different from all the other peoples on the earth. In this the prophecy of Jeremiah was absolutely fulfilled:

"The time is coming," declares the Lord, "when I will make a new covenant with the house of Israel and with the house of Judah. It will not be like the covenant I made with their forefathers when I took them by the hand to lead them out of Egypt, because they broke my covenant, though I was a husband to them," declares the Lord. "This is the covenant that I will make with the house of Israel after that time," declares the Lord.

"I will put my law in their minds and write it on their hearts. I will be their God, and they will be my people. No longer will a man teach his neighbour, or a man his brother, saying, 'Know the Lord,' because they will all know me, from the least of them to the greatest," declares the Lord. "For I will forgive their wickedness and will remember their sins no more."

(Jer. 31: 31-34).

Unlike the old People of God, who needed to be differentiated from the world as, for instance, they kept a special 'Sabbath Day', the new People of God did not need such differentiation. Christians, in fact, soon realised their need to break with the old traditional Sabbath, and began by meeting on the first day of the week, and not the seventh, in order to worship their risen Lord. In fact they did not need any legalistic prohibitions as a basis for their relationship with their heavenly Father because, as St Paul rightly stated, "He who loves his fellow man has fulfilled the law" (Rom. 13: 8-10).

It is also important to grasp that God's people were not essentially to be marked out from the world by the dogmas they believed (although right belief is important), nor by having a particular kind of establishment or bureaucracy. They were certainly also not ultimately to be distinguished by a particular mode of worship (although Jesus did institute the "Lord's Supper"). The real hallmark of their life was that they loved the God and Father of our Lord Jesus Christ, with all their heart, mind, soul and strength and that they "loved their brethren" to the uttermost.

John Wesley saw this in the eighteenth century when he said that the "people called Methodists" had been raised up by God to spread scriptural holiness as "perfect love". It was indeed the Methodists' love for each other which drew the working-class people of the industrial revolution into their community in such large numbers. In fact, the saying "See how these Christians love one another" should be the cry of the world in every age because in the end "perfect love" for God and each other is, basically, what the healed Christian community is all about.

It has been a thrilling experience for my wife and myself to see in our day that same expression of love within Christian communities which have been truly renewed by the Holy Spirit. Indeed, such acts of mercy have been commonplace. We saw it, for instance, in the willingness of ordinary believers in our church at Hainault to take drug addicts and even prostitutes into their homes, in order to help them towards rehabilitation. I can also well remember one of our people actually taking his jacket and new coat off his back in order to give them to a new convert who had been a down-and-out tramp. We saw the same Spirit at work in the people of St Luke's,

Seattle, when moving testimonies were frequently given by out-of-work church members about how they and their families had been enabled to keep sheltered, warm and fed by the unsolicited gifts of fellow members. In many cases the "givers" had indeed helped the others, to the point of real self-sacrifice. If such acts of charity are needed, and can be freely given in two such wealthy countries as Britain and the USA, then we can easily see how magnetic the love of the Christian community was in the harsh realities of poverty in the Roman empire of the first century AD.

It perhaps took some time before Christians realised that they could, and should, love the people "in the world", without actually embracing their standards and godlessness. They needed the further guidance of the Holy Spirit to see that Paul's exhortation to come out and be separate from the world (2 Cor. 6: 17) did not mean that pagans should not be the objects of their love.

It was Jesus Himself, however, who obviously first taught that practical expressions of love should go out to the needy and that this love should cross all social, racial and even religious divisions. It is difficult for us who have inherited many centuries of tradition of all-embracing Christian love, to realise just how shocking to its hearers was the parable of the Good Samaritan. It was here that Jesus defined the neighbour that God had commanded His people to love as "anyone in need". In that very parable He also taught how easy it was for the "religious" priest and Levite to miss out on real love, through a false piety. Jesus subtly turned the scribe's question: "Who is my neighbour?" upon the questioner himself by implying "Are you yourself neighbourly, as was this Samaritan?" (Luke 10: 29-37). Jesus' words, "Go and do likewise" have certainly rung out throughout the Christian community in all ages, as the ultimate in fulfilling the law of love.

From this study of Christian love, I find it impossible to agree, however, with the view of many radical Christians today, that God's people, as an outworking of their love, should be engaged in programmes to change the very structure of society. On the contrary, it seems to me that Jesus accepted the structure of society in which He lived and did not advocate changing it by either political or military activity. It seems also that the New Testament writers likewise taught submission to the structure of the society in which they lived (*e.g.* Rom. 13), to the domestic structure which included the subordination of women (Eph. 5.22), and even to the existence of slavery (1 Pet. 2. 18 etc).

However, it can be said that the meaning of love as seen and practised by the Christian community has always had within it the motive and the power to bring about social change, wherever injustice exists. So Richard Foster, in his admirable book *A Celebration of Discipline*, points out that the law of love, as it was understood by early Christians, would not be difficult to work out for such people as women and slaves, or even the poor; for they were already in the position of under-dogs in the first century. The main difference for such Christians would be one of attitude, as through their love for God, and from their status as His sons and daughters, they could willingly yield to their masters in true submission. However, as Foster points out, the concept of 'agapë love', the love of God and for God and for one another flowing within the Christian community, is surely that "salt" which seasons the whole, or that "leaven", or yeast, which lightens the lump of the whole society. In this age, therefore, as much as in any previous one, the Christian community is meant to recognise, embody and minister all that love truly is, so that the world may believe that God was in Christ reconciling the world to Himself, and human beings to one another.

Chapter 29
Christian wholeness and witness to the world

The teaching of both Jesus and the apostles was that the Church, the new People of God, can never exist for its own sake. Jesus, having called the Christian community into existence, left it with the command:

"Therefore go and make disciples of all nations, baptising them in the name of the Father and of the Son and of the Holy Spirit, and teaching them to obey everything I have commanded you."

(Matt. 28: 19-20)

He promised them the power to fulfil this mission when He said:

"But you will receive power when the Holy Spirit comes on you; and you will be my witnesses in Jerusalem, and in all Judea and Samaria, and to the ends of the earth."

(Acts 1: 8)

This mission began on that memorable day:

When the day of Pentecost came, they were all together in one place. Suddenly a sound like the blowing of a violent wind came from heaven and filled the whole house where they were sitting. They saw what seemed to be tongues of fire that separated and came to rest on each of them. All of them were filled with the Holy Spirit and began to speak in other tongues as the Spirit enabled them.:

(Acts 2: 1-4)

Almost immediately we find Peter out in the streets proclaiming to the Jews that "God has raised this Jesus to life, and we are all witnesses of the fact" (Acts 2: 32) and that "about three thousand were added to their number that day" (Acts 2: 41).

The reason for the Church's existence is nowhere put more explicitly than in the words of St Peter himself. when he wrote:

201

> *But you are a chosen people, a royal priesthood, a holy*
> *nation, a people belonging to God, that you may declare*
> *the praises of him who called you out of darkness into his*
> *wonderful light.*

(1 Pet. 2: 9)

However, as the Christian community began to fulfil the command of its Lord, they soon began to suffer persecution, and in so doing learned further the meaning of His words when He had said:

> *"If anyone would come after me, he must deny himself*
> *and take up his cross and follow me. For whoever wants to*
> *save his life will lose it, but whoever loses his life for me and*
> *for the gospel will save it."*

(Mark 8: 34-35)

The Church, therefore, if it is to be true to its calling, can never be a community that seeks to preserve its life or even perpetuate its own existence. It can never be a bureaucracy, an entity or an organisation which is ever seeking to expand itself. It cannot be forever counting heads or numbering those who belong. This, in fact, had been the problem which God had had with His old Covenant people, the Jews; they were overly concerned about their own existence and clung onto what they had of God and His laws. Eventually they even became complacent about the fact that He would protect them, their land, the Holy City of Jerusalem and the Temple in which He had chosen to meet with His people. They refused to give away their life and the knowledge of God to other peoples. They put a protective boundary around themselves and, to their horror, saw it all smashed down by the heathen, and only a remnant remaining to witness to the glory of God.

By the time of Jesus, this remnant was reduced to one: Jesus himself, as "He came unto his own, and his own

202

received him not" (John 1: 11, *AV*). The new People of God began to come into being as Jesus called the twelve to Himself. Their numbers were multiplied as others began to believe on His name. The first Christians were conscious that their message was "first for the Jew" (Rom. 1: 16), but as these people still refused to believe, apostles like Paul would shake the dust off their feet against them and turn to the Gentiles (Acts 13: 46-48).

Luke, in his history of the early Church, is keen to point out that the Lord added to their number daily those who were being saved (Acts 2: 47). It is apparent, however, from both Acts and the epistles that the New Testament believers were always willing to lay down their lives for the faith in their risen Lord. They let nothing obstruct their mission, even death itself. They left such matters as the growth or otherwise of the Church in the hands of the Lord. That they saw as His business; theirs was the proclamation of the gospel.

It is true, throughout the centuries of church history, that when the Christian community has become over concerned about its life as an organisation and sought the expansion of its power and influence as a bureaucracy, its life has decayed. Even today, whenever the efforts of Christians are motivated by such desires as "to get them to church", to "fill empty pews" or to "get money for the maintenance of the organisation", their endeavours prove self-destructive.

Even many who have sincerely belonged to the Lord have, through the centuries, reacted against the establishment, finding it difficult to see any relationship between the life and words of Jesus of Nazareth and the pomp, glamour, pride of position and exertion of power in such institutions as the Roman Catholic Church or the Church of England. Perhaps it is for this reason that the greatest expansion of Christianity in the world today lies hidden in multitudes of meetings for praise and worship in believers' homes. Such gatherings are often under the leadership of men who are engaged in secular occupations, and certainly have none of the trappings of the traditional clergy.

This same feature of the mission of the Church today was seen especially in the Communist countries. There the established church was easily recognised and therefore could be brought under the control of the political regime. However, it was the underground church with its lay pastors which spread most rapidly, and posed the most threat, and was therefore constantly the object of persecution by the State. Nevertheless, it would be inaccurate to paint too gloomy a picture of the established Church in what were Communist countries or, for that matter, any other nation. It has certainly not been rejected by God out of hand.

There are, within its life, many faithful believers who see that the church, so manifested, still has an important role to play in the nation in which it was created. It is because of their continual response to new movements of the Holy Spirit to purge and revitalise His Church, that reforms are introduced and the "faith once delivered to the saints" is still maintained. They feel it right to maintain their place in the institutional Church in order to be a prophetic voice to it.

Sadly, many such renewed Christians have felt conscience bound to leave historic denominations, only to find in subsequent years that they have fallen into the same error and produced yet another denomination which has basically the same faults as the one they left - an urgent desire to formalise, protect and preserve its own life! Thankfully the Holy Spirit continues, in this as in every age, to point Christian communities back to the fact that they are primarily called by the Lord to be His witnesses.

It is important, therefore, if we are able to be faithful to the Lord in our generation, that we ever keep before us the nature of the task to which we have been called as Christians. This is to bear witness to the life, resurrection and present Lordship of Jesus of Nazareth, who is the ultimate revelation of God's judgement and love, the be-all and end-all of creation. Further, a witness is a person who has seen, heard or touched something or someone, and who (like the Samaritans of the Gospel story) can say, we believe, "for we have heard for ourselves, and we know that this man really is the Saviour of the world" (John 4: 42).

To take a simple illustration: if the police today were asking for witnesses to an accident, they would not be satisfied by the evidence of people who were imparting only second- or third-hand information. They would, however, be relieved to find and take statements from those who could say, "I was there and I saw it myself". So Christians are called upon to share their own experience of Jesus with those in the world with whom they are in contact. They must, like the man delivered from evil spirits, go and tell how much Jesus has done for them (Luke 8: 37-39). If they do not do this, under the impetus and guidance of the Holy Spirit, then they are failing in the main purpose for which they themselves were brought to know the Lord.

If we follow the evidence of the New Testament script-ures, however, we find that Christians always bore their witness to Christ **very conscious of the fact that they were expressing the life and function of the Christian community as a whole.** Life in the community, in fact, was basic to their own personal witness. The reason for this was manifold. Most importantly, however, every individual Christian knew that it was only through the existence of the Church that they had ever heard of Jesus and therefore been 'born again' and able to respond to Him. They were conscious of the fact that the existence of the community bore a corporate witness to the Lordship of Jesus. They realised how fallible individual, personal experience could be. They knew that they could have been deluded or deceived, or even imagined that Jesus was with them, if they alone in the world were convinced that He had risen from the dead. It was for this reason that Jesus at first appeared to His disciples when they were together, and thus they had a corporate experience of Him as risen Lord. For this reason also Paul later emphasised again the fact that Jesus was seen by believers who were together, even five hundred of them at once, when he was seeking in his letter to reconvince some members of the Corinthian Church that the Lord had been resurrected.

So, even if, as in the case of Philip (Acts 8), the act of witnessing seems to have been that of a solitary person, this was only a temporary state of affairs, and Philip knew that his own testimony to Christ had arisen within and was supported by the whole Christian community. It is interesting to note that Philip's solitary witness to Jesus, in Samaria before the arrival of the apostles from Jerusalem, was supported by another important factor in evangelism, that of "signs and wonders". We read that the Samaritans, when they

> heard Philip and saw the miraculous signs he did, they all paid close attention to what he said. With shrieks, evil spirits came out of many, and many paralytics and cripples were healed. So there was great joy in that city. (Acts 8: 6-8)

These events take us back to the preaching of Peter himself, which followed the sign which was done through the healing. of a lame man (Acts 3), and to the urgent prayer of the early church: "enable Your servants to speak Your word with great boldness. Stretch out Your hand to heal and perform miraculous signs and wonders through the name of Your holy servant Jesus" (Acts 4: 29-30).

Here, as in many places in Acts, we see the way in which miracles of healing and deliverance from evil spirits, in the name of Jesus of Nazareth, bore witness to His continued life and Lordship. The world recognised that a dead, crucified man couldn't still be healing the sick. Jesus was risen! They not only heard, but saw this was true!

It is most important to realise that when such men as Paul, Barnabas and Silas went out on their missionary journeys, it was with the laying on of hands in blessing by the Christian community. They went, in fact, not only as representatives of the Lord Jesus Christ Himself, but as representatives of His Church. Their task was not only to lead individual unbelievers to faith in Christ, but to establish like communities of faith in every town where people would acknowledge their witness to be true.

It is important also to see that the witness of the Christian community to the Lordship of Jesus of Nazareth was not carried on in a haphazard manner. On the other hand, there was no purely rationally worked-out strategy. The Church sought, in all things, to be directed by the Holy Spirit. So the early Christian community sought corporate guidance from God. This was so in matters such as the separating of Paul and Barnabas for their missionary journey (Acts 13: 2), or in critical decisions which had to be made about rules of conduct for the new, Gentile churches. In all things they wanted to be able to state that "it seemed good to the Holy Spirit, and to us" (Acts 15: 28).

207

There are recorded in Acts various other ways by which the Christian community, as a corporate body, sought to witness to the reality of the risen Christ, besides the spoken word and the working of miracles in His name. They no doubt did so by their joy, which led to worship, praise and thanksgiving to the Lord, even in the midst of terrible hardships and persecutions (Acts 16. 23). They certainly did so by the willingness of their members actually to lay down their lives for their Lord. The witness of Stephen is especially significant in this respect, as it was almost certainly a vital factor in the conversion of Saul of Tarsus, the persecutor, into St Paul the missionary (Acts 8-9). It is also specifically mentioned, in the early record, that the love and care of the community for each other was a witness to the presence of the Lord amongst them:

> *All the believers were together and had everything in common. Selling their possessions and goods, they gave to anyone as he had need. Every day they continued to meet together in the temple courts. They broke bread in their homes and ate together with glad and sincere hearts, praising God and enjoying the favour of all the people. And the Lord added to their number daily those who were being saved.*

(Acts 2: 44-47)

In all these, and in fact in every act of witness, we are called to remember the primacy of the Church, the Body of Christ. This is so even when a Christian may, geographically, be entirely on his own, when sharing his testimony with another person. It may seem rather flippant, but it is nevertheless a very meaningful illustration of this truth when I tell congregations I have been invited to address, that "I decided to bring my body with me". I could, I tell them, have decided only to be with them "in spirit", but that, knowing they wanted "me", my body was indispensable. My body is, I explain, the visible, tangible representation of me, through which we can communicate with each other. So Paul told the Corinthian Church that they were, **corporately**, the Body of Christ, and that each one of them was, as an individual, a member (an organ) of the Body (1 Cor. 12: 27). In other words, the Corinthian Church was the visible representation of Jesus Christ in that area. It was only through their life, as a "body", that the people of Corinth would see and hear Jesus.

In this connection, we do well to remember that there were two main factors in the person of Christ as recorded in the Gospels: the power of His ministry, and the beauty of His character. These are represented respectively by the gifts and the fruit of the Holy Spirit at work in each Christian community. The same truth holds good today. The world, amidst all its chaos and confusion; all its lack of direction, is crying out to see Jesus. Mankind in the twenty-first, as in the first century, will only see Him as His power and beauty are displayed by His Body, the Church, with every member endowed by the Spirit, fulfilling his or her particular role both within it and as an emissary of it.

So the people of God are today called to every aspect of witnessing to the salvation wrought by Jesus Christ, their living Lord, in the all too secular society of the twenty-first century. Thankfully, as the forces of darkness have sought to increase their grip on modern man, through his blindness in the face of his eternal origin and destiny, seeking to bring him to total destruction, so the Holy Spirit has also been moving amongst His people in great power. He is even now at work re-creating His Church, a confessing Church, which is bearing witness to its Lord, even leading to death. May God ever guard it from the perils of self-preservation, of building again an edifice which has to exist because it is afraid to let go of life and trust its Lord. He died, giving up His life, in love for His fellows, and God raised Him from the dead to the place of ultimate glory. His Church must obediently follow Him, laying down its life for the world, endeavouring only to seek and to save that which is lost. In so doing, it will follow its Lord, through death to life. Like a grain of wheat it must fall into the ground of secular society and die, and in so doing it will bring forth much fruit. It will lie "in dust, life's glory dead", and from the ground there will "blossom red, life that shall endless be" (G. Matheson).

This is the way the Master trod; shall not His servants tread it still?

Epilogue
My personal trial of faith

Anne and I launched out in an itinerant worldwide ministry of evangelism, healing and spiritual renewal in September 1975. We began to live by faith. I had had five years of very intensive and demanding ministry as vicar of St Paul's, Hainault, near London, and now we had a very full diary of ministry ahead of us, involving a great deal of travel. I was sustained throughout this almost incredibly draining work, and became pastor of St Luke's Episcopal Church, Seattle, USA, in 1981. I had hoped that ceasing to travel would be less demanding, as I was feeling extremely tired. However, the work at St Luke's proved to be just as involving as St Paul's, and once again the calls came to us to go to different parts of the USA on mission. It was whilst engaging in one of these missions that I collapsed, at Dallas, Texas, and was hospitalised in Seattle completely and utterly worn out.

I was told by the doctor that I was a burnt-out man who had put three lifetimes of work into one. I had severe chest pains, and although I was discharged from hospital I kept being rushed back by ambulance as an emergency case. I was also suffering from deep depression and phobic illnesses which, I was told, was the result of a massive chemical imbalance brought about by sheer overwork. Eventually I realised I could no longer carry on at St Luke's, and doctors told me that I would be an invalid for the rest of my life. I was given medication for my heart problem and was told that I would have to take it for the rest of my life, otherwise I would soon die. I was pensioned off by the Episcopal Church of America, the Church of England and British Social Security, and returned to England in March 1983.

I spent most of my time in bed, as a physical and emotional wreck. Then one day my eye lighted upon a verse in Psalm 118. It read:

I shall not die but live, and declare the works of the Lord.

This scripture came to me as a bolt from heaven, and I knew that it was a direct word from God to my stricken state of health. I immediately had the witness in my spirit that I was being healed by the power of God's word, giving me the confidence to throw all my heart tablets away; and I have never had a chest pain from that day to the present time. I felt that I was going to be immediately healed by God, just as I had been as a teenager. It was then that what Peter calls in his first letter "a trial of faith" really began (1 Peter 1: 6-7).

Although I had no further chest pains and knew my heart had been healed in such a way as if it had never been sick (a fact verified by medical examination), the depression just would not lift. I felt to be in a pit of despair. I received the laying on of hands so frequently that it's a wonder I didn't go bald! I went through healing of memories so deeply it's a wonder I didn't forget who I was! I even went to a deliverance centre to see if I had picked up a demon, but they knocked at the door of my soul and nothing evil answered.

At times I felt somewhat better and, in faith, arranged Christian meetings, only to find I immediately lapsed into exhaustion, depression and fear. I cried out time and time again to the Lord; I tried to meditate on His word; I tried resting in the loving arms of the Lord. I found I could not pray. The heavens seemed like brass, and I began to wonder, in depression, if God really existed at all. All this time my wonderful wife nursed me, worried about me, prayed for me, ministered to me, encouraged me. Over a hundred people covenanted to pray for me. I hung on; it was a **trial of faith**, because I believed God cared and would heal me – but when? and how?

These bouts of intense depression lasted fourteen years – fourteen long years – and then the Lord did it – quietly and undramatically and even without direct ministry, yet surely in response to our prayers, including those of the many who joined together in praying for me on 22nd July, 1996. I woke up one morning and knew that I knew: that I knew I had been healed – not by any new medication – but by the Lord Himself.

A trial of faith is when we are trusting God for healing – maybe doing everything taught in this book – but prayer isn't answered; healing does not come. Peter said:

These (trials) have come so that your faith – of greater worth than gold, which perishes even though refined by fire – may be proved genuine and may result in praise, glory and honour when Jesus Christ is revealed.

(! Peter 1: 7)

I do not know why God waited so long to heal me. All I know is that I have emerged, Anne tells me, "more loving, more sympathetic, more patient, more kind, more gentle," and, as she paid me these compliments, she added: "You have become a wonderful man." Those who have known my ministry tell me also that it is deeper, more sensitive, more gentle, more profound and yet more powerful, all to the glory of God.

Perhaps. dear reader, you are going through a trial of faith. Learn from my experience: keep believing, trusting, praying and hoping – and when you can't do that – lie back in the comfort of the everlasting arms. God, our Heavenly Father, is about the business of making us whole, even sometimes through pain and suffering; spirit first, then soul, then body; all are important to Him; and He is the master physician – very good at His job.

APPENDIX A
Christian healing
and the world of medicine

Although in Bible times the science of medicine and the work of the physician were, compared to today, very primitive, it may be helpful to consider how they have been regarded by the people of God. A definition of medicine is: "The art or science of prevention and cure of disease; any substance which safely helps to bring about this end".

There are several Biblical texts concerning medicine:

> *A cheerful heart is good medicine*
>
> (Proverbs 17: 22)

Balm was a form of medicine. Jeremiah wrote:

> *Is there no balm in Gilead? Is there no physician there?*
> *Why then is there no healing for the wound of my people?*
>
> (Jer. 8: 22)

and:

> *"Go up to Gilead and get balm,*
>   *O Virgin Daughter of Egypt.*
> *But you multiply remedies in vain;*
>   *there is no healing for you."*
>
> (Jer. 46: 11)

Isaiah gave this advice for the King's healing:

> *"Prepare a poultice of figs."* *They did so and applied it to the boil, and he recovered.*
>
> (2 Kings 20: 7)

In the New Testament Jesus said:

> *"He (the Samaritan) went to him and bandaged his wounds, pouring on oil and wine."*
>
> (Luke 10: 34)

Oil and wine were used in those days as medicines. And Paul gave the following advice to Timothy:

214

. . . use a little wine because of your stomach and your frequent illnesses.

(1 Tim. 5: 23)

When we turn to the Biblical mention of physicians, in the Old Testament 'Rapha' and in the New Testament 'iatroi', we find that the ministry of the physician was regarded as very different from that of the sorcerer, enchanter, witch, charmer, wizard, necromancer or a consulter with familiar spirits. All the latter were forbidden occultists in the Old Testament (Deut. 18: 9-13), but the use of a physician was not barred to God's people and is not mentioned in the list of banned ministries.

In the Old Testament God took upon Himself the title of 'Physician' when He declared to Moses:

"I am the Lord thy Physician" (Exodus 15: 26 *NASV*).

In Genesis Chapter 50 it is recorded that

the physicians embalmed Israel (Gen. 50: 2).

Job said to his so-called comforters:

"you are worthless physicians, all of you!" (Job 13: 4).

And it is said of King Asa that

he did not seek help from the Lord, but only from the physicians. (2 Chron. 16: 12)

In the New Testament Jesus gave tacit approval to the ministry of physicians when He said:

"It is not the healthy who need a doctor, but the sick."

(Matt. 9: 12; Mark 2: 17)

but of a woman who came to Jesus for healing it is said:

She had suffered a great deal under the care of many doctors (Mark 5: 26) and *she had spent all she had on doctors* (Luke 8: 43);

and in Luke Chapter 4 we find, written as a proverb:

"Physician, heal yourself!" (Luke 4: 23)

It is very important to note that Luke, who wrote the Acts of the Apostles as well as the Gospel, travelled with

215

Paul and was probably a physician to him and his co-workers. Paul calls him the "beloved physician" (Col. 4: 14). He was with Paul on several of his missionary journeys (Acts 16:10-17; 20:6-12, 14-Ch. 28:16).

So we see that overall there is a uniformly good relationship between physicians and the spiritual people of both the Old and New Testaments, and that "primitive" medicines were accepted as valid means of healing for God's people. This has become clear as we have considered Joseph's, Jeremiah's, Jesus' and Paul's attitude to the work of physicians.

Even though the science of medicine has advanced very considerably since New Testament days and the range of preventative measures such as immunisations, surgery and curative medicine has progressed such that today a great many illnesses can be healed or alleviated, and also, if not able to cure a sickness can relieve a lot of pain and distress, nevertheless medicine is not in any way related to the healing of the spirit from sin. This is a purely spiritual action performed by the Holy Spirit, springing from the work of Jesus on the cross in the ways I have described. Medicine does not or should not engage in any spiritual ministry at all.

Further, although drugs have now been produced that can *sometimes* alleviate sickness of the soul, such as depression, in my vast experience of dealing with this need I have come to the conclusion that although modern medicine can treat such illness through the action of chemicals on the brain and nervous system, they very rarely can *cure* it. However, through the ways I have described, God **can and does do it.**

The science of medicine is at its best when it is addressed to the sickness of the body, and Christians can prayerfully and wisely avail themselves of their doctors'

The science of medicine is at its best when it is addressed to the sickness of the body, and Christians can prayerfully and wisely avail themselves of their doctors' services to this end, seeing their work as an extension of God's providence in the realm of healing. However, there are very many common illnesses which medical science can still not really *heal*, and it is true to say that man's extremity is God's opportunity, for "All things are possible with God."

Many Christians have felt **called by God** to be doctors, surgeons, nurses and engage in other related professions at home and abroad as means of serving Him for the alleviation of suffering in our fallen world, and these are to be commended.

However, Christians should beware of forms of "alternative medicine", as most have occult origins or base their treatments on pagan philosophies. Obviously, as considerable research has revealed, a healthy diet and exercise are very helpful in preventing and curing many sicknesses. Christians would do well to take note of all the good educational aids now available for healthy eating.

A good physician uses the **scientific** – not magical – method, using God's natural laws, whilst those in Divine Healing ministry use God's spiritual laws to return people to health. Both can work happily together.

(I am indebted to Dr Rodney Curtis, a General Practitioner in Matlock, Derbyshire, who is a Christian doctor and who also believes in Divine Healing, for some of these thoughts and teaching.)

APPENDIX B
Some reasons
why seekers are not healed

In this book I have taught from Biblical evidence that it is God's perfect will that His people should be completely whole, totally healed until the moment when, in His timing, it is His will to take them to be with Himself in heavenly glory. Even this transition to heavenly life is, however, limited to this dispensation of Grace; for when the Lord returns in splendour to fully establish His Kingdom, then death itself shall be no more a power to engulf those who belong to the Lord. In the meantime, I have shown the ways in which God moves, through His Holy Spirit, to heal spirit, soul, and body. However, despite all this provision, some of God's people remain unhealed. In this final appendix I shall examine at least some of the reasons why this is so.

God's healing is not magical and, as we have seen, He has made the receipt of it absolutely dependent on faith. The faith which brings God's healing into a sufferer's life is not a common commodity. This is because, especially in Western society, the whole teaching of our scientific and technological culture militates against the possibility of miracles occurring. The vast majority of us have been schooled in this negative teaching since our earliest years, and it pervades the spiritual atmosphere in which we live. Evangelists constantly report many more remarkable miracles happening in more "underdeveloped" countries than occur, say, in England; this is because believers there are more ready to believe in God's power to heal and accept it without question.

Jesus Himself could not do many mighty miracles in His home town of Nazareth because of their unbelief, or lack of faith (Matt. 13: 58). Unbelief pervaded the minds of those in that town. It was almost "in the air", and it must be said that we, in the West, not only live in an unbelieving society, but, sad to say, the Christian Church itself is full of unbelief in the area of the miraculous. I experienced many mighty miracles through my ministry in my parish church at Hainault 1970-75 because I ministered Divine healing in a climate of expectant faith on the part of the congregation. There, Divine healing ministry was far from being just another ritual, as it is in some churches where I have ministered. The congregation expected miracles to happen!

We must add to this teaching on the necessity of faith to bring healing from God the very important fact that those who **minister** healing must themselves have faith that what they say and pray for **is** going to happen; otherwise they should not minister to the sick at all, because they are being grossly unfair to them.

Then finally in this respect, there must be faith in God's ability to heal and His will to do so, on the part of the recipient of ministry. Such faith must not be confused with 'hope' or sincerity. As James says in his letter:

> But when he asks, he must believe and not doubt, because he who doubts is like a wave of the sea, blown and tossed about by the wind. That man should not think he will receive anything from the Lord

(James 1: 5-7).

So doubt is perhaps the greatest barrier of all to the receipt of healing from God.

Another barrier to Divine healing is the absence of a complete, utter and absolute desire to be a whole person, declare oneself to be so, and live without any artificial props or attention, with full responsibility for one's life as a totally well person. Such a desire was not taken for granted by Jesus, who once asked a very incapacitated man if he really wanted to be well (John 5: 6). Even if a sick person seems actually to be seeking healing, there can still be an unconscious holding on to the sickness which prevents a total return to health.

Then, as we have seen, sin; lack of obedience to God and His commands, or deliberate, wilful violation of the standards of the Christian life, with lack of repentance or willingness to make reparation and amend one's life, can be barriers preventing God's healing power reaching us. There is also the failure to restore broken relationships, or such things as hidden, deep down bitterness and resentment which will hinder our healing by God. All these blockages are on the part of the seeker.

There is still, however, what I consider to be a major factor as to why we do not see, as we should, the mighty works of Jesus being done on a widespread scale in our day. This is because the ministry of Jesus was **perfect**. He was a completely whole, sinless, and perfect vessel for the Father to use. He was more full of the Holy Spirit than perhaps most of us can ever hope to be. He also had perfect discernment and knowledge as to the cause of a person's sickness; whether it be sin, a fever or a demon, and today's ministers often lack such perfect discernment in dealing with each individual who is sick in different and particular ways. Those of us who minister today have this treasure "in earthen vessels", and our ministries are far from perfect. We offer ourselves as the best we can be, to be used by God, to become as clean vessels as we can, minister in obedience to His Word, and, praise Him, we give Him all the glory for the many miracles which, spirit. This was so in the case of Paul's "thorn in the flesh". It was indeed an angel of Satan that was "tormenting" him. He sought the Lord more than once for an end to this suffering, but was told:

"My grace is sufficient for you, for my power is made perfect in weakness." (2 Cor. 12: 7-10)

Despite all the hindrances to God's healing power, praise Him that He still gets through to us and it is His will, in His time and by His methods, to make us totally whole.

"Faithful is He who calls you, who indeed will do it."

(1 Thess. 5: 24)